HEALING FOR YOU

A moving account of a healer's background, development and work.

HEALING FOR YOU

The story of Phil Edwardes a healer with remarkable power

by

PHIL EDWARDES
AND
JAMES McCONNELL

THORSONS PUBLISHERS LIMITED
Wellingborough, Northamptonshire

First published 1985

British Library Cataloguing in Publication Data

McConnell, James
Healing for you.
1. Faith-cure
I. Title II. Edwardes, Phil
615.8'52 RZ400

ISBN 0-7225-0939-1

Printed and bound in Great Britain

Contents

'Through the centuries healing has been practised by folk healers who are guided by traditional wisdom that sees illness as a disorder of the whole person, involving not only the patient's body but his mind, his self-image, his dependence on the physical and social environment, as well as his relation to the cosmos.'

Prince Charles, addressing the
British Medical Association
on its 150th anniversary in December 1982.

This Book . . .

If you suffer in mind or body this book can be of help to you. It may do more than that, it may transform your life and your whole attitude to living. Maybe you yourself are in fine shape mentally and physically but you know someone who suffers greatly or who has sunk into despair. This book may enable you to help them. For its message is that pain and suffering can be relieved when all the normal remedies have failed.

'Healing' is a word which is not easily defined. In the simplest terms it means the alleviation of disease through the laying on of hands. The healer transmits a power which comes from beyond him, passes through him to the patient and in most cases brings a significant betterment, sometimes a cure that appears miraculous. In the pages that follow you will read about the life and work of one healer. His name is Phil Edwardes. He lives in the Sussex countryside and in all respects except one is a reassuringly normal family man. What makes him different is that he possesses the gift of healing to an extraordinary degree.

Healing is often referred to as paranormal. We tend to shy away from the paranormal, as we do from the occult. We forget that paranormal simply means 'alongside the normal' and that occult means 'hidden', or 'hid from our sight'. We do not shrink from a peace 'which passeth all understanding' nor do we shiver at the statement that faith is 'the evidence of things not seen'. Why then should we reject healing because it baffles our limited comprehension? Healing is indeed an aspect of the paranormal, but a most wonderful and reassuring aspect.

We do not understand why there is disease in the world but we can see that much of it is unnecessary. Many illnesses are avoidable and most will yield to healing. Some sufferers are sceptical of healing, others think that they are not worthy to receive such a blessing. Many feel that they lack the necessary faith. There are even some who in their heart of hearts do not wish to be freed from their illness. Healing however is available to all, irrespective of their beliefs.

Healing is nothing new. The early years of Christianity were known as the Charismatic Era. During that time miracles of healing were performed not only by Jesus but by his disciples as well. Their purpose, we are told, was to prove that He was the Messiah, and when that message was firmly established the miracles ceased. But healing is by no means a prerogative of Christianity. It transcends religions, races and creeds. There are healers on every continent and in every land.

If healing is symptomatic of a charismatic era we are living in one now. Wonderful things are being done in Britain today by the men and women who have this God-given gift. Phil Edwardes however stands out as a healer endowed with remarkable and exceptional power. His methods are very much his own, and are characterized by the time and the care he devotes to each individual. In this he is different from healers who deal rapidly with a succession of patients or who conduct mass healings with a large audience. He is essentially modest, taking none of the credit for himself. Yet the observer inevitably feels that the role of the healer is very important, since it is he who acts as the channel for a power which we cannot understand.

A great change is taking place today in attitudes of mind about such things. People are turning away from the purely materialistic approach. They are showing more readiness to accept truths that cannot be scientifically proven and striving to recover knowledge that has been lost. It is noticeable how many people you meet now who are interested in some aspect of what we call the paranormal. Surprisingly, this change of attitude is shared by many nuclear physicists and in particular by the researchers who are exploring the universe within the atom. There is a remarkable similarity between the latest theories of Western sub-atomic scientists on the nature of the cosmos and the conclusions drawn by Eastern mystics thousands of years ago.

The medical profession too is at last reaching out towards those forms of medicine which are usually described as 'alternative'.

The fact that doctors prefer to call them 'complementary' is a sign that they foresee a collaboration between themselves and properly accredited practitioners of complementary medicine. Healers such as Phil Edwardes would welcome a closer association with orthodox medicine, which every day achieves thousands of marvellous cures. Although healing has often been effective where more normal methods have failed it can also complement or reinforce the efforts of doctors. In many of the examples cited in this book doctors have approved the recourse to the healer. Now, medical men have set up a Research Council for Complementary Medicine; it has a similar standing to the Medical Research Council.

In so many ways ours is an age of fear, for man's scientific advance has given him the means to destroy the world he lives in. The fear is a real one and many lives are overshadowed by the dread of a coming holocaust. But remember that there is another side to scientific advance. Man has made his puny leap to the moon and has devised ever more powerful telescopes to pursue the fleeing galaxies. Now he is turning his attention more and more to the universe within him. That will be the direction of the next great advance in human knowledge. Healing is a pointer to those uncharted regions.

If you suffer from any disease, be it mental or physical, which will not yield to medical treatment why not accept that a wonderful gift is available and may be bestowed on *you?* Read what the healer himself has to say about healing, then read the stories, wonderful stories, of people who have received healing through him. The same healing is available to you and the experience may open a door onto a whole new concept of life.

Foreword

by Dr Priscilla Noble-Mathews B.M., O.St.J.

Medicine is the science and art of healing. Broadly, there are two forms of healing.

The first occurs through Divine intervention to bring about healing which is totally above (but not against) the nature or the natural gifts of man. This is the true miracle.

The second, natural healing, is the process by which the body's own healing mechanisms (about some of which we know very little) are stimulated into action. It comes about when man uses his natural, God given, gifts, when he utilizes all his skills to extract from his environment those things which are beneficial for him. He may draw on the plant world, from the fields of biology, physics and chemistry, from those things which can be explained in physical terms to those which at present are outside the ring of tangibility and explanation in terms of current thinking and knowledge.

In all these fields man uses his hands — to dig plants, to design and use the tools, to focus the microscope, to hold the electromagnet or the laser, to wield the scalpel, to touch the computer and to write down his findings.

The hands of a man are among his most vital gifts. We talk of people who are good with plants as having 'green fingers'. Is it, therefore, so surprising that he should be able to make use of his hands directly for healing?

In earlier days it was the art of medicine which was practised and malpractised, construed and misconstrued. Gradually the balance of the pendulum has tipped towards the arm of science until today medicine is equated almost solely with science, often in its coldest form of observed material facts. But science itself, by its very name, is also responsible for gathering knowledge.

Orthodox medicine regards itself as the guardian and arbiter of health, therefore it carries a great responsibility. In the discharge of this responsibility it often appears to be more concerned with protecting patients from those confidence tricksters, who undoubtedly exist, rather than with its positive vital function of drawing good from all possible fields for the ultimate benefit of mankind.

One needs to remember, moreover, that man is not a purely material being. Medicine must look at the patient as a whole and this means that a proportion of our care for patients is not going to fall neatly into the realm of hard fact which can be measured scientifically.

Sir Robert Platt said:

> Some clinical problems can be solved by knowledge, some by experience and some by understanding. The application of these three qualities has come to be known as clinical insinct or clinical wisdom.

In other words we come back to the balance between the science and art of healing.

This book is about the life of one person and the moments that the lives of certain others were touched through his. It tells the story of a man who discovered that through his hands healing could occur. It relates the experience of some of those who came to him. These people tell their own stories in their own words. The strict use of medical terms is therefore not to be expected, but after many orthodox consultations few patients describe their condition exactly as the doctors think they have communicated it to them.

In this particular field of hand healing, since these patients found help, is there not something here worth taking seriously and observing more closely? That would be for clinical research and this book must be a strong pointer to the need for it.

Perhaps in our present state of knowledge we may not be able to explain 'how', but we can observe and record, at least to explore whether or not a process claimed to occur does so in fact. Time enough then to push back further the frontiers of science in our never ending search for all the means by which we are enabled to 'cure our patients sometimes, alleviate them often and comfort them always'.

Prelude

When you meet June you have an immediate impression of healthiness and enjoyment of life. She is in her early forties and walks gracefully, almost athletically. Her face, her eyes are smiling, her complexion is rosy. She has a natural infectious laugh.

She and her husband live in Sussex at Stringer's Cottage, Thakeham. Max is a civil engineer and works for the Water Authority. His spare-time interest is weapons and their role in military history. They have a son aged nineteen who is at a polytechnic in the North, and a daughter of eighteen who does a secretarial job in Horsham. Two bouncing Airedales complete the household.

You would never guess that a couple of years ago she was in the depths of despair, an incurable cripple hobbling round the house in constant acute pain. Now she sits snugly in a deep armchair while she talks, her legs curled underneath her. Or she moves lithely to put more logs on the fire, then sits on the low stool by the hearth. She smiles often and laughs with pleasure as she tells a story that shatters preconceived ideas about the human condition.

She was only four-and-a-half when her left knee was attacked by tuberculosis. She was living at Newcastle on Tyne at that time and thinks that she was infected by cow's milk. In the 1940s TB was often a fatal disease, for the drugs we have now had not been discovered. From the age of four-and-a-half till she was seven June was confined to a sanatorium. During the first months her infected knee became rigid and bent more and more. She could do no more than hobble because her legs were of different lengths.

There was only one available remedy. Her surgeon straightened the knee by giving it a sudden wrench. The pain was agonizing as she was not under anaesthetic. She was put in plaster from ankle to armpit. The plaster was gradually removed till it only covered her knee. But the knee remained in plaster for two more years.

When the plaster was finally removed her knee was fixed in a slightly bent position. On the day she was discharged both her parents came to take her home. She left the hospital on crutches. Her mother had been told that June would never be able to walk without support.

June, however, had decided for herself that she would walk normally again. Even as a child she had great determination, and walk she did. But the knee was fixed in a permanently bent position and it remained like that till 1980. This disability did not prevent her from living a normal life. She grew up, got married, had children.

In September 1979, she was on holiday with her family in Northumberland. Fording a river, she slipped on rounded slippery stones. Her legs went from under her and she fell, striking the base of her spine on a rock. At the time she thought she was only winded, but later a huge bruise appeared on her back. Back home in Sussex she began to become aware of a pain in her left leg. It got worse and worse. She went to see her doctor.

He examined her and told her that she had bruised her hip. He prescribed pain-killers, advised her to 'take things easy'.

During the next month the pain became really severe. She was on a whole succession of different pain-killers. Then, driving the car in Worthing one day, her leg completely packed up and she narrowly escaped an accident.

She told her doctor that she wanted to have an X-ray. He refused, but added that he did not object to her seeking a second opinion. She asked to be transferred to his partner, a woman doctor. It was a providential decision, though at the time June had no inkling of what the outcome would be.

Her new GP read her notes and immediately decided she must have an X-ray. Christmas arrived before the results. On Boxing Day she collapsed. She felt very ill and found it almost impossible to move. She spent three days in bed but forced herself to get up and go to keep her appointment at the doctor's surgery.

The X-rays showed that she had compounded three vertebrae at the base of the spine and at least two discs were out. That she was walking at all was extraordinary.

She asked the doctor whether there was anything that could be done. The reply was no. The sciatic nerve was trapped. The only hope was that if she lay flat on her back for a few weeks the inflammation might go down.

As she could not make the journey to hospital and no NHS physiotherapist was available to make home visits, she had to have private physiotherapy. But it was to no avail. Her doctor was worried and perplexed. She took various blood tests — for rheumatoid arthritis, for the liver, for cancer of the bone — and arranged for June to go into hospital for two weeks under the care of the rheumatologist.

She was given hydrotherapy and traction. To stretch her spine in an effort to untrap the sciatic nerve a tension of ninety pounds was applied. After two weeks she was discharged with instructions to attend the out-patients' department for further traction.

The first time she went back was not a happy experience and the physiotherapy did not improve her leg. She felt very bad on the way home in the hospital car. The next day was a horror story. June's memories of it are understandably confused and there were moments about which she cannot bring herself to talk even now.

The trauma began at 7 a.m. when she wanted to go to the toilet. She tried to slide out of bed using the technique she had been taught. A searing pain lanced her. She fell onto the floor and got stuck there, kneeling with her arms on the bed. The slightest move caused white-hot agony.

Max rang the private physiotherapist. It was eleven o'clock before she arrived. By that time June had been on the floor four hours. The physiotherapist managed to lift the screaming June into bed and tried to force the sciatic nerve back into place. 'A bad experience' is June's only comment.

Her GP came at twelve-thirty. She agreed that June was a case for hospitalization, but the specialist who had dealt with the case was on holiday and it was four o'clock before Max succeeded in talking to his 'locum'. When he heard what the situation was he dropped everything and dashed out to Stringer's Cottage. By that time June was delirious with pain. She was into ague and sweating profusely.

'He was a good man,' June said of the locum. 'He confirmed that the sciatic nerve had come adrift. He twisted my leg into a contortionist position and somehow succeeded in forcing the sciatic nerve into place.'

Next he commanded her to sit up, then stand up. She did so. It was an old-fashioned remedy, he confided, and did not always work.

She was in bed for two weeks. A surgical corset had been prescribed but wearing it was unendurable; it pressed on the sciatic nerve. She went back to her rheumatologist at Worthing. Could they not do some operation, anything to free her from this dreadful pain? The chances of success were less than forty per cent, the specialist told her. He could not offer that way out.

'There I was, back at home but in tremendous pain. I could lift nothing, not even a tray. I was shuffling from room to room in desperation, taking lots of pain-killers every day.'

In the end her body began to reject the pain-killers. She sank into blank despair. There seemed to be no way out, no help at all.

Calling in one Saturday morning, her GP found her in this state. She was deeply concerned for her patient.

'I don't know, love. There's nothing more the medical profession can do for you. But you can't go on like this.' She hesitated before coming out with what was in her mind. She was a compassionate woman with strong religious convictions. Though dedicated to her own profession she had some knowledge of another kind of therapy. 'I don't say this to everyone, but — would you accept any other form of medicine?'

Gradually June realized that she was talking about Healing.

'You mean a faith healer, a spiritual healer?'

'No,' the doctor corrected her. 'A healer.'

June was sceptical but ready to try anything. She agreed to go and see Phil Edwardes, a healer who lived near Wisborough Green.

Max was even more sceptical when she told him about it. Who had ever heard of a doctor referring a patient to a healer? In his heart of hearts he believed that the last lot of blood tests had shown the presence of cancer and the doctor did not want to tell them.

It was on 4 June 1980 that he helped his wife out to the car. Getting her into the passenger's seat was quite a performance as she could not bend at the waist. The seat was tilted back so he could not secure her with the safety belt. He packed her in with about eight cushions. Once on the road he drove as gingerly as if he was transporting a consignment of fine crystal. Every jolt caused June to wince.

The drive was only about eight miles but to her it seemed like eighty. Phil Edwardes' house was one of a group on the Billingshurst-Loxwood road. A short avenue led up to the gravelled parking space. In the garden the roses were in bloom but she had no eyes for the beauties of nature. Opposite the front door of the house was a single-storey building hung with baskets of scarlet trailing geraniums.

The good-looking man who came out to greet them was tall, well over six foot. He had the build of a back-row rugby forward and his smile was attractive and reassuring. He was dressed casually in a pullover, open-necked shirt and fawn slacks. He seemed about ten years older than June, say around fifty. He was clean-shaven with dark hair cut very short. He had a strong jaw and thoughtful, friendly eyes. His hands were expressive, with long sensitive fingers.

Max found his appearance and manner reassuring. He seemed very straight, with no hocus-pocus about him and a direct way of looking at you.

Together the two men supported June into the converted coach-house. Phil Edwardes helped her to get settled in a chair in the waiting-room.

'Do you mind if I smoke?' he asked, somewhat to her surprise.

'No — no. Not at all.'

Phil produced a pack of cigarettes and lit up.

'Now, tell me what the trouble is.'

She realized that her doctor had not passed on any details but had left June to tell him about her illness.

'I heal nobody,' he explained when she had finished. 'I am only the channel through which healing flows and I can't tell whether I'll be able to heal you or not till I try.'

June had no feelings either way. She was willing to give it a chance but had no real confidence that this charming but perfectly ordinary man could do anything for her. She let herself be helped into the room opening off the waiting-room. After the car journey every movement was painful but she had become accustomed to pain. She sat on a square, highish stool, facing the single window and looked out at a rushy pond with trees and sky beyond.

Phil Edwardes was behind her. He put some quiet music on the cassette player. He had told her that all she needed to do was just relax. The music helped her to do that. After a while she was aware that he was standing behind her. His hands were at her shoulders, then her head. They barely touched her but she could feel them trembling, sort of fluttering.

The only feeling she had was one of peace.

It lasted about ten minutes, she could not be sure of the time. The music stopped. He came round and leaned an elbow on the window-sill, looking down on her.

'Well, how do you feel?'

She had felt nothing at all. There had been no apocalyptic experience, no visions in the sky, just this vague feeling of peace.

'There's healing for you,' Phil said. 'I'm sure of that.'

She mumbled some non-committal words and got off the stool. Phil accompanied her out through the waiting-room. Max, standing by the car outside, seemed surprised.

'How did it go?'

She was starting to tell Max that it had been a non-event when she saw that both men were smiling. She realized with a shock that she had walked out without help.

Most wonderful of all, *the pain had gone!* For the first time in months she was free of pain. That alone was more, far more than she had dared to hope for.

A little dazed, she got into the car, already less dependent on help and able to sit upright. Now she was smiling too. Freed from pain she was again seeing the world as a beautiful place.

'Same time next week?' Phil enquired tentatively.

She nodded. Deep down she knew that this man was going to heal her completely.

On the drive home she and Max did not say much, but once inside their own front door they hugged each other with joy. Something tremendous had happened, but what? How could you explain something like that? And what sort of man was this Phil Edwardes, who had been able to banish her pain without even touching her?

A Healer's Life and Work

by Phil Edwardes

There is only one religion, the religion of love.
There is only one language, the language of the heart.
There is only one caste, the caste of humanity.

Sai Baba

Birth of a rebel

Expert gardeners will sometimes take the root and trunk of a common, hardy rose and graft onto it a more lovely and more beautiful bloom. The lower part is called the stock and the flowering portion is known as the scion. My growth has been like that. I am a very common or garden fellow but late in life I found that I could be the instrument of a most wonderful power — the power of healing.

Not till I was forty-seven did I become a healer. There had been signs as long as twenty years earlier but I was not prepared to recognize them. I never really aspired to be a healer. I did not believe that anyone so flawed as me could have this gift. I resisted till eight years ago when something happened which forced me to face the reality. Only then did I understand the meaning and purpose of my existence.

The life I led up till 1977 is hardly of significance to anyone. But it serves to show that the designer who created us does not discriminate when he needs a channel for his healing love. Looking back I can see that events which at the time I regarded as misfortunes played their part in leading me to where I am now. So, if you will bear with me, I'd like to take you briefly through my first forty-seven years, up to the time when the scion was grafted onto the stock.

My beginnings were not quite as obscure as the character in Oscar Wilde's play who was born 'in a handbag, at Victoria Station', but very nearly so. I was born a bastard. I mean that literally. I was forty-eight before I discovered the circumstances of my birth. Even then I could not find out much. My mother did not want me. She was living near Romsey when the baby that was to be me became due. She went up to London and took a room in a lodging house. It was part of a Victorian terrace somewhere in Mayfair. She only stayed there a fortnight after I was born before going back to Romsey. As for me, I was carted off in an open car driven by a man with red hair. And that's all I know about my arrival in the world.

My earliest memories go back to the age of three. By then I was living at Yew Lodge, a big Victorian house at Havant, near Portsmouth. It was the home of Mrs Edwardes, who had taken me into her care after I was abandoned by my mother. I grew up knowing her as Mama. Her father had been an admiral in the Royal Navy and her husband Captain of HMS Canterbury, whose ship's bell now hangs in Canterbury Cathedral and is struck every day in remembrance of the men who perished at sea. At some time in her life she had been a Member of the Court of St James. Many decades later I wondered whether this was a clue to the reason why she took me into her family.

She had a son and daughter of her own, and to supplement a meagre service pension she boarded the children of parents whose jobs took them away from England for long periods. She was a small woman with a very forceful character. She lived by strict Victorian standards and ruled the herd of children by those same standards. Her discipline was firm but loving. And I loved her in return.

Meals were strictly supervised. If one of us was guilty of bad manners Mama would lean forward and administer a sharp rap on the knuckles. Every Sunday we had to go to church. Mama would sit in the row behind and if one of us so much as coughed she would lean forward and give the offender a whack on the shoulder with her umbrella.

I did not resent Mama's strict régime. It was my experiences at boarding school that turned me into a rebel.

I was only seven when I was sent to Emsworth House and the wrench of leaving Mama and Yew Lodge was very great. I never discovered how my education was paid for. All three schools I attended were independent but I cannot say that the money was well spent.

From my memories of Emsworth House one stands out vividly. I was in the common room with a number of other boys one day. No doubt we were ragging about but I was not conscious of doing anything naughty. Suddenly a master appeared. Sweeping through the room he picked on me and grabbed me by the scruff of the neck. He took me into the next room, made me bend over and gave me a thrashing with a cane. It was a very painful and unpleasant experience. I never knew what my offence had been. That was probably the moment when the spirit of rebellion was born in me.

In 1939, aged nine, I went on to Fernden School. For the first time I became aware what a social stigma it was to be illegitimate. Somehow the other boys had found out about it and they were very cruel in their mockery. I was dubbed 'Oik Edwardes'.

The name stuck when I went on to Sherborne in Dorset. I know it is one of the best public schools but the war was on and standards had gone down. By now I was a confirmed rebel. Rules meant little to me and I was always coming up against the system. I had little enthusiasm for organized team games and absolutely no ambition to get into the sixth form. It was made very clear to me that there was something unacceptable about me.

'Edwardes,' a master said to me, 'you'll end up as a crossing-sweeper, that's all you're good for.'

Looking back on my public school days, I think that what scarred me most was the religious teaching and the sermons in chapel. The Divinity classes reinforced my feeling that I was a lost cause. The sermons led me to believe that I myself was the product of wickedness and vice — Oik Edwardes, the bastard. If all these preachings were true I had precious little hope in this world and a damn sight less in the world to come.

There are always two sides to a coin. My instinct told me that all this talk of damnation and hell-fire could not be right. In a way this is what saved me, for my rejection of the accepted doctrines led me to do my own questioning. I set out to try and discover for myself about such fundamental matters as the nature of the creation, the purpose of human existence and man's relationship with the deity.

Jack of all trades

When at last I was free of school it was 1946 and National Service was still in operation. The armed forces with their regimentation were not for me. I joined the Palestine Police. Palestine was then under a British Mandate. There was a lot of shooting going on at the time as the age-old rivalry between Jews and Arabs flared up. I spent most of my eighteen months as a constable patrolling the docks at Haifa, armed with whatever weapon was suitable for the job — revolver, rifle, Tommy-gun or machine-gun.

By 1948 I had done my stint of National Service and returned to England. I applied for a job with the Metropolitan Police and actually passed the entrance exam. But in the meantime the Palestine Police Resettlement Office had got me a job in the Rhodesian Police. I went out to Northern Rhodesia and served as a sub-inspector first at Mufulera and then at Broken Hill. I did not stick it for long. The tedious paperwork, the routine, my supervisor's insistence on petty aspects of discipline brought out the rebel in me and I quit.

My next job was on the railway that ran from Northern to Southern Rhodesia. Its purpose was to serve the mines and carry away the minerals and precious metals that came out of them. There was something of the old Wild West about Broken Hill in those days and Roy Walensky was its most colourful figure. He had been a railway fireman and then a driver and still lived in one of the houses provided by the railway for its employees. He was a constant visitor to the Railway Club and I once had the distinction of playing whisky poker with him there.

I started as a trainee fireman. The work was hard but it had its rewarding moments. More skill than you'd think goes into firing a steam locomotive. That's why a fireman's shovel becomes as precious to him as an infantryman's rifle. There is a great art in keeping the bed of red-hot coals at just the right thickness and temperature. You have to maintain a thin bed to avoid clinker. You have to synchronize it to the gradients of the railway line, for the engine needs more steam going up hill than down. It was a matter of pride never to have such a surplus of steam that it had to be blown off in a great white cloud. The driver can make a lot of difference to your life, too. If he's clumsy or takes a dislike to you he can waste your steam and double your work.

There were usually a few of us trainees on an engine for these long runs. During periods off duty it was good to leave the cab and go up to the front of the great cylindrical locomotive, clinging to the hand-rail, as it roared through the night at over a hundred miles an hour. I used to love sitting at the front above the cow catcher with the gale rushing against my face, the headlamp slashing the darkness and the vast landscape of Africa stretching away to the left and right. Then, back in the cab, we would crack an egg and fry it on a shovel hot from the furnace.

I enjoyed that time of my life. It was a lot of fun. The work was hard but the food was good and I slept like a log. The pay was generous and even as a trainee fireman I had an African servant. That way I earned the only qualification I possess. I ended up as a fully qualified Railway Steam Locomotive Fireman.

My behaviour, however, was too riotous for the railway company and they gave me the sack. I'm afraid that's the kind of fellow I was in those days.

I went down to Salisbury, the capital of Southern Rhodesia, and was lucky to get a job as a bus driver on the urban routes. I held it for six months. The crunch came one day when I was careering down a hill that led onto a bridge. I swiped a car waiting to cross the opposite way. It was my bad luck that its occupant was the head of the company that insured all the city's buses. As that was my fifth accident in four months I was asked, not unreasonably, to resign.

After a spell as a meter reader for the electricity company I joined up with a friend and we went out to live rough in the bush. Under the stars I had a chance to think. I was twenty-one, my life seemed aimless and I was getting nowhere. I decided to return home to England.

That was easier said than done. I boarded the train for Cape Town but only got as far as Mafeking. The South African Police, terrifying men as tall as pylons, did not like the look of my beard, sun-blackened visage, bush hat and beat-up leather jacket. I had no onward ticket from Cape Town and they made that an excuse to send me packing back to Salisbury.

I shaved the beard off, bought some new clothes and a ticket to England and tried again. This time I made it past Mafeking and reached Cape Town a fortnight later.

'Coming home', as all the Brits in Southern Africa called it, did not really solve my problems. I continued to lead as aimless and rudderless a life as in Africa, drifting from job to job — clerk to a brewery, forestry worker, farm trainee, salesman to a firm of seed manufacturers. The most useful thing I did was play Rugby for Chichester and then Petersfield. As I was 6′1″ and weighed 13 stone I was in demand as a back-row forward.

It was in 1959 that an incident occurred which made a big impression on me. It stood out from the negative aspect of my life at that time as something positive and worthwhile.

I was walking beside a lake near Kineton in Warwickshire when I noticed something floating in the water about thirty yards out. It was just near enough for me to realize that it was a woman. She was alive but making no attempt to swim. I flung off my shoes and jacket, dived into the water and swam out to put into action the life-saving techniques I'd learned in the baths at school. It was lucky I was a strong swimmer. That woman did not want to be rescued. She fought me desperately and I had my work cut out to get her to the shore. Even then she tried to throw herself back in the water and I had to restrain her till help arrived.

I visited her later in hospital and learned that it was the loneliness of bereavement that had led her to such a desperate action. Since her husband's death she could see no purpose in going on living. All the same she was grateful. It had been an impulsive action and she was glad I'd come along and hauled her out. She must have made a good story of it because some time later I received an Honorary Testimonial, on vellum, from the Royal Humane Society. It was something to add to my certificate as a Railway Steam Locomotive Fireman.

In 1960 two things happened which gave more direction to my life. I met Ann, who was soon to become my wife, and I got my first job in the trade which was to be my occupation for the next seventeen years. I started in the motor trade as a second-hand car salesman in Basingstoke, but it was not long before I was appointed relief manager, working out of the Blue Star Garage in Newbury.

Then I had a lucky break. A friend of mine by the name of Mike Engel was on the sales side of an oil company. Through his influence I got the tenancy of a garage and service station at Bucks Green, not far from Horsham. The business prospered and by 1967 we had made enough money to acquire the lease of a garage near Gatwick Airport and six months later another at Chessington.

Life had been so hectic during those years that we had little time to spare for finding a suitable home. But when Roundstreet House came on the market I knew as soon as I saw it that this was the place for me. It was within easy reach of Bucks Green, it was in the country, though not far from the attractive village of Wisborough Green, and it had a nice garden just the right size. I have always been particularly fond of roses and this garden was full of them.

The oldest part of the house dated back to Tudor times. There was something attractive about the way the rooms were laid out at different levels. A quirky staircase of very old timber led upwards from a flagged hall. A feature that intrigued me was the study on the left as you came in. A staircase in one corner of it led up to a large landing, in itself a small room. I saw this as a future library, lined with books. There was a large sitting-room, a dining-room, two bathrooms and plenty of bedrooms. Opposite the front door was an old coach-house, a useful brick building with a tiled roof. Above all, the house had a welcoming feel about it. Just the place to bring a wife and five kids.

After the usual delays contracts were exchanged and we moved in during the summer of 1967. At last my life seemed to have settled down into an organized pattern. My family were delighted to be living in the country. Business was booming at the Gatwick garage, where we were providing off-airport parking as well as petrol sales and servicing facilities.

Then an event occurred which changed everything.

Blood ties

Phillip, my second son, really thrived on this new life. At the age of nine he was two years ahead of his contemporaries at school. And this was not only in academic work. He came out as *victor ludorum* competing against boys of thirteen. Amongst his group he was the natural leader and perhaps this was the reason for the touch of arrogance which was his only fault.

Across the road from our house is a minor road that leads down to a few farms and houses. Beyond a cattle grid there is a winding hill where an old oak stands. On a summer's day in 1970 Phillip and some friends went cycling down this track. As usual Phillip was in the lead, head down to reduce wind resistance. The tractor coming up the hill was being driven by an elderly learner-driver. In a mistaken effort to avoid the boys he drove across the track onto the grass verge on the right-hand side. Phillip's head struck the tractor, now careering out of control. Before the old man could stop it, a back and a front wheel ran over his chest.

Phillip was still lying unconscious on the track when I reached the spot. The sight of him was a terrible and unforgettable shock. He was rushed to hospital in Guildford and taken into intensive care. He was X-rayed and examined by two doctors. He had suffered extensive brain damage and severe internal injuries. Neither of the doctors thought that he could live. All that we could do now was wait.

Though I was shattered by this news I personally did not give up hope. And at this point I must forewarn the reader that what follows may be difficult to believe. But I am only relating what happened, exactly as it happened and as I experienced it.

Though not a spiritualist myself I had been in contact with spiritualists during the early years of my marriage to Ann when we were living in Banbury. I did not quite share their views but I had learned a lot from them. This had led me on to joining a discussion group which was interested in paranormal subjects. I had also made friends with some spiritual healers who lived in Oxford.

When I'd heard what the doctors had to say I immediately telephoned these friends in Oxford. I told them about what had happened to Phillip and described his present condition. I asked them to give him absent healing — sometimes known as distant healing.

All that night I sat by the bedside of my unconscious son. In the early hours he vomited a little dried blood. When the same doctors came in the morning they seemed surprised that he was still alive. Further X-rays were taken with a portable machine. The doctors were puzzled. An hour later they returned and took another X-ray. The internal injuries had disappeared overnight! The only signs of damage now were the large bruised areas on his arms and shoulders and the scoring of the flesh on his chest. The doctors were at a loss to account for his amazing recovery. I knew that this was the power of absent healing, but I kept my counsel.

Phillip did not regain consciousness for three weeks. During that period my friends in Oxford continued to direct absent healing to him. When at last he did come round Phillip was far from normal. The personality which emerged from the long coma was changed. One felt that he had brought back with him the atmosphere of a very beautiful place.

When he returned home he had to learn to walk all over again and learn to ride a bike from scratch. Whereas before he had been inclined to arrogance he was now very sensitive to other people's moods. And he could not bear conflict of any kind, for instance the sound of other children squabbling.

Ann and I would not accept the fact that his brain damage was permanent. We were sure that he'd become normal again. But it took a long time, years. There was no school that he could fit into and he went from one to another. He had forgotten all about the rules and regulations of a school and it was not exactly helpful that he showed no respect at all for the masters. During classes he would get up and wander about, or go and talk to the lady who cleaned the school. In a way he was living in another world, but with it all he was a lovable and loving person. By the age of sixteen 'Gentle Phil', as he was called, was holding down a minor job in a factory in Billingshurst.

But that's looking ahead. It is never easy to talk about the failure of a marriage. The reasons are always too complex and intimate to be shared with the outside world. All I want to say is that after ten years of marriage it had become obvious that Ann and I were incompatible. We were slowly destroying each other and there was only one solution to the increasing unhappiness and stress. We agreed to separate, though Ann continued to play an important role in the life of the children.

There was another big gap in my life. On my thirty-fifth birthday I had lost Mama, the one person in the world whom I could look on as a parent. She died on 25 October 1965. The loss of her affected me keenly. During the years that followed I began to feel more and more a need to know something about the family I'd sprung from. I wanted to clear up the question of my parentage and birth. It is strange how much a thing like that can matter. It's a deep human need to know by whose agency you came into this world and until you find out you have a sense that somehow you don't belong.

I was already into my forties when I at last decided to do something about it.

Mama had explained to me, as soon as I was old enough to understand, that I was not really her son. I'd often asked her who I really was, who were my parents, why my family had not wanted me. My questions seemed to upset her, and I could not understand why she always avoided them. I sensed some mystery there.

The Salvation Army has a department in London for tracing people, especially the parents of children who have lost touch with their families. They have a lot of resources and plenty of experience and they provide the service free. So I started off by going to them.

It took them a little time but eventually they let me know that they had succeeded in tracing my mother. For some reason they would not tell me who she was or where to find her. Here was another mystery.

I bided my time and started to put money into a savings fund. When I had enough I engaged a private detective agency to take up the search. After a couple of months they reported to me that they had found the register of my birth at Somerset House. My father's surname had been entered as Seymour, the name I'd been given when I first went to Yew Lodge. It turned out to be false. My grandfather's name was Stride. The agency had been able to trace my mother's last known address. It was at a place called Nursling Mill, near Romsey in Hampshire.

I was at Barwell Motors in Chessington when I heard the news. I jumped straight into a car and drove down to Romsey. I was able to locate the site of Nursling Mill. It was on the Test to the east of Romsey, just outside the town. But the mill itself had vanished, long since abandoned.

Tramping the fields in my business suit I met a farmer who had worked in this neighbourhood since a boy. Yes, he remembered Nursling Mill and the woman who had lived there. And he'd known of the Strides, a well-to-do family with a house on the Test and a fine stretch of fishing. There were two daughters, he remembered. Good-looking lasses. One of them had married a solicitor in Romsey, name of Swayne, and when old man Stride died she'd inherited half his fortune. There'd been a son by that marriage. Henry. Ten years older than me, he'd be. As to other children, he didn't know. He had not seen her for years but he'd heard tell that she was still living in Romsey. Yes, it so happened that he did know the address.

It turned out to be a detached house on the outskirts of the town. I felt both nervous and excited as I stood on the doorstep waiting for my knock to be answered. In a few minutes I'd be looking at the mother who had brought me into the world.

The door was opened by a woman who could not have been more than fifty. She was not nearly old enough to have been my mother. Her look of surprise quickly changed. She stared at me as if she thought she must have met me somewhere.

'My name's Edwardes,' I said. 'Could I have a few words with the lady who lives here — an elderly lady?'

I hoped that the briefcase I was carrying would support my story that I had some business to discuss with the 'elderly lady'. But my cover was already blown.

'I know who you are,' she said, in a voice that was not unfriendly. 'You're Henry's younger brother — aren't you?'

'Yes,' I admitted.

'He's often wondered what became of you.' She was still studying my face. 'You're very like him, you know.'

'Are you — ?' I started, wondering if this woman could be a sister of mine.

'Oh, I'm sorry! I should have explained. I'm Beth, Henry's wife. Come in and I'll 'phone Henry. He works in Romsey.'

It took Henry less than ten minutes to hurry back from his office. His appearance provided a rough specification of what I could expect to look like in ten years' time.

The conversation which followed was a curious one, to say the least. At last I steered it round to the subject of my mother.

She was in a downstairs room, Beth told me. I caught the look she exchanged with Henry and realized that the subject was painful to them.

'Could I see her?'

Again that quick exchange of glances.

'She's very old, you understand,' Henry said. 'Her mind's gone. I don't think she'll recognize you — even if she remembers anything about you.'

'I'd still like to see her.'

Beth led me down a passage, opened a door and left me to go in on my own. Entering the bedroom I had a strong sense of unreality. This was the moment I had been looking forward to for so long and now that it had come my feelings were frozen.

The room was dark and close. It was obvious that the woman in the bed was in the early stages of senile decay. The eyes that turned towards me were blank and disinterested. I could feel neither resentment nor tenderness towards her. But I very badly wanted her to know who I was.

'I'm your son,' I said. There was no other clue I could give her for at that time I still knew nothing about the circumstances of my birth. 'Do you remember – forty years ago?'

It meant nothing to her. Talking to her was very difficult and it took me a long time to get anything through to her. In the end she seemed to realize vaguely who I was, but about my father she could tell me nothing. Her mind wandered away and further conversation became pointless. I left her to her ramblings and quietly closed the door. I never saw her again.

From my half-brother I learned that my father had owned a garage in Southampton – an odd coincidence. He did not know anything more about him, but he was able to tell me that just before my birth my mother had gone up to London for a couple of weeks. 'Mummy is sick,' he had been told. Her secrecy was understandable since Henry's father was not my father. Not till years later did she tell him that he had a half-brother somewhere in the world.

'That farmer I met,' I said. 'He told me that people from London used to come down and stay at the house of my mother's parents. Mama – I mean Mrs Edwardes who brought me up – was a Member of the Court of St James. Do you think there's any connection? I mean, could that be the explanation why she sort of adopted me, and my education got paid for?'

'I couldn't say,' Henry replied. 'But did you know you had a sister?'

So it was that I learned I had a sister, a real sister with the same mother and father. Her name was Pam and she lived with her husband in Southend. She had four children, the last only a few weeks old.

That information made the whole quest worthwhile.

It was some days before I was able to drive to Southend. Pam lived in a terraced house with a small postage-stamp garden. The door was opened by a lovely young woman ten years younger than me.

I said: 'Are you Pam?'

'Yes.'

'I'm your brother.'

I had felt nothing when I saw my mother but this meeting was deeply emotional, at the same time painful and thrilling. I had at last found someone to whom I really belonged through blood ties. It may be hard for those who have always had the security of a family background to understand how much this meant. Though we were strangers we quickly found that we had great affinity. We saw things in the same way. Pam had a warm-hearted approach to people and I found I could respond to her open personality.

Later she and her family moved to Crawley, quite near to us. Pam was a trained nurse and got a job as matron of a nursing-home there. We were able to see a lot of each other and our relationship grew deeper and deeper. We never made any effort to trace our father. There seemed little point and, besides, the garage he owned, as well as the municipal records, had gone up in the blitz on Southampton. Nor could she tell me any more than Henry had about the mystery of my 'adoption' by Mama and the funding of my education.

When, some time later, we heard that our mother had died, we felt no real grief. The important thing was that late in life we had each found kith and kin — she a brother and I a sister.

Garage man — or Healer?

The Gatwick garage was now so profitable that I had given up both the other garages to concentrate my efforts on the off-airport parking business. At that time the volume of traffic at Gatwick was building up and we were in great demand from travellers who wanted their cars garaged while they were abroad. We would take them to Departure and pick them up at Arrival when they returned. Many of them wanted their cars serviced or repaired during their absence. We provided a twenty-four-hour service and gruelling work it was. A short week was 80 hours and on some weeks I was working up to 120 hours. There were days when I did not get home till two in the morning and was off again at seven.

My right-hand person in this mammoth task was a young woman of about twenty who had worked for me since the Bucks Green days. Her name was Sue. She was a glutton for work, not only doing the books but driving the mini-bus, selling petrol, dealing with the staff and their pay, cleaning the loos — you name it.

Working so closely with Sue I came to appreciate her marvellous qualities. Having recently been through the painful experience of a failed marriage I was hesitant about entering into any new commitment, but as time went on I realized that I had at last found the perfect partner. We became engaged, and in due course married. So Sue came to fill the gap left at Roundstreet House by the departure of Ann.

It was really thanks to an initiative of Sue's that something happened which caused me to completely change my way of life.

I had for a long time been interested in the paranormal. In the days when I was a seed salesman living at Banbury I had been a member of a discussion group. We were not irresponsible dabblers in the occult but serious and dedicated people in search of knowledge and understanding. When I moved to Newbury another group used to meet in my flat to discuss paranormal subjects. One of its members was Percy Corbett, who later became secretary of the Church's Fellowship for Psychic and Spiritual Studies.

I was sitting one evening in my favourite chair with the others round me. It's an old craftsman-built wooden chair with a high back and arm-rests and it stands today in the healing room at Roundstreet. All at once I felt as it were an electric current pulsing down my arms. The power seemed to originate somewhere behind me. My hands were tingling so much that it would not have surprised me to see sparks coming from the tips of my fingers.

I told the others what I was feeling. We all joined hands to see what would happen. Immediately they all felt the same thing, like an electric charge going through their bodies.

Even Percy Corbett could not account for this. It did not occur to any of them that it might be connected with a healing power — certainly not to me. I knew that there were healers but I assumed they must be people of high character who led blameless lives. Not Oik Edwardes, born a bastard, whose only qualification was as a Railway Steam Locomotive Fireman.

Nonetheless, experiences like that increased my interest in things beyond the normal. In the years that followed I had contact with a number of sensitives — or mediums, as they are sometimes called. Some very strange things happened, but this is a book about healing and not spiritualism, so I will only say that they altered my views on such fundamental things as life and death. I now had evidence that physical death did not extinguish life. So, I reasoned, there must be some purpose in living. The religious teaching at school had led me to associate

God with judgement, damnation and hell-fire. Now I had become convinced that, in spite of appearances to the contrary, a loving design lies behind human and cosmic existence. This implied a loving designer. The word 'God' was for me bound up with doctrines I could not accept. That is why I prefer to speak of the creator spirit as 'the Guv'nor'. Not till many years had passed was I to realize that I had a part to play in his grand design.

During my early days as a garage manager I had been given an indication that I might have a healing power, but I still shied away from it. When I was at the Blue Star Garage at Basingstoke there was an RAC patrolman by the name of Charlie Woods who used us as a regular port of call. He would drop in for a cup of tea and we'd often sit and chat about the ways of the world and Timbers' problems with his duodenum.

One day he came in clasping his belly and grimacing with pain.

'God, my stomach's killing me!'

'Something disagree with you, Timbers?'

'No, mate, I'm getting it all the time now. Can't keep anything down. Nights I can't sleep, my stomach's so sore I can't even bear to touch it. It's them ulcers. My doctor's given me pills, ought to make it better but they don't do no good.'

While he was talking I felt heat in my hands. I had experienced this before but had not connected it with any healing power.

I said quite casually: 'Have you thought of going to a healer like Harry Edwards? He has a big house near Guildford where people go to be healed.'

'Edwards? Any relation of yours?'

'No. We spell our names differently. He's healed a lot of people.'

'A healer? No, I never thought of that. What's a healer do?'

The heat was still in my hands but I did not want to say anything about that. I certainly was not going to claim that I had any healing power in me. All the same I felt I wanted to do something about Charlie Woods.

I said: 'Sometimes the healer has to put his hands on you. Like this. Put your hand on the table, Timbers.'

He put his hand on the table. I held my own about twelve inches over it.

'Can you feel anything?'

'Your hands! They're hot!'

'That's healing,' I said and went on to talk about something else.

Charlie Woods was amazed but at the time neither of us put great significance on it. You'd expect healing to be carried out in a church or somewhere by a bloke in a white surplice, not by a garage manager in the dingy little office at the back of the workshop. Charlie went on his way and I forgot all about it.

Three weeks later he turned up again. He was a different man. His face was cheerful and smiling and he was thumping his stomach as he came in.

'I don't know what you did, Phil, but you cured the trouble.'

My mind was on automobile repairs and I did not immediately grasp what he meant.

'My stomach!' he said. 'You did the trick. The pain's gone and I'm sleeping nights, can eat what I like now. Had a steak last night and it went down a treat. None of those pains that used to nearly kill me.'

Stomach ulcers, even I knew this, are often caused by worry and stress, sometimes anxiety or fear. Perhaps something else had occurred to take a load off Timbers' mind. I did not really think that I was responsible.

Later I had more direct evidence and I might have acted on it if I had not received what seemed like a rebuff.

Soon after I'd moved to Bucks Green I got to know a young lad of sixteen who suffered from very severe curvature of the spine. It was really double curvature because his spine was bent in an S-shape, and locked in that position. There was a hump where his spine went behind one shoulder-blade. He had to get about on crutches because his legs were withered. Orthodox treatment was not helping. I persuaded him to let me take him to see Harry Edwards.

Harry Edwards sat him on a low, square stool. He called me over. He made me put my hand on the injured part of my friend's back. Then he put his own hand over mine. I felt the boy's vertebrae move under my hand. He stood up straightened. The hump had gone. He was not able to walk out of there without his crutches but from that day forward his spine was straight. Oddly, he never went back for more healing.

Back at home I wrote to Harry Edwards to tell him what I had experienced. I never received a reply.

Early in the summer of 1977 Sue and I were having lunch at a pub not far from home. Sue began to chat to the woman behind the food bar. She was interested in the practice of yoga, but some problems had cropped up which were troubling. Sue invited her to come to Roundstreet for a talk. She thought that perhaps I could be of some help to her.

She arrived the following Sunday with a friend she introduced as Maria. We were in the sitting-room discussing the problem when Sue noticed that Maria was sitting on the edge of the sofa, very uncomfortable and awkward.

'It's this allergy,' Maria explained, and thereupon she turned her back and pulled up her T-shirt. The lower part of her back was in a terrible state. I can only describe it as like raw steak.

Her doctor, she explained, had not yet discovered what was causing the allergy, so she was not receiving treatment for it.

Looking at her back I began to feel that odd sensation in my hands which I now associate with healing — a kind of trembling and tingling plus a feeling of heat. I wanted to touch Maria's back.

I got up and asked her to keep still. Then I placed my fingertips on the small of her back. I could feel the healing pouring through my hands. It lasted for several seconds.

'What's happening?' Maria asked.

'I think you're getting some healing. Just keep still.'

'What's healing?'

'Never mind.'

She kept still and waited. My fingers were shaking slightly but I hardly touched her back. Later she told me that during those moments she had an extraordinary sensation, 'as if my whole inside was being shaken up'. When the healing sensation stopped I went back to my seat.

By next morning all Maria's pain had gone and the rawness was healed. Her skin was flaky as if recovering from sunburn. Soon it was completely back to normal.

After the incident with Maria I made up my mind to go and see a healer named M. H. Tester who lived at Haywards Heath. I had read his book and knew his reputation. He gave me an appointment and I went to see him. He listened in silence to what I told him.

'Phil, you're a healer,' he said. 'Get on with it.'

Fan-tastic!

Tester's words gave me the push I needed but it was largely due to Sue's encouragement that I decided to give it a try. I had put it off for long enough. Looking back I sometimes wonder if I wasted twenty years of my life. But perhaps the Guv'nor knew I was not ready to start working for him till now. It was only recently that I had discovered about my roots and had at last found a sister who was blood of my blood. And I now had as a helpmate someone who understood what sort of person I really was and supported me to the hilt.

Though the Gatwick operation was booming it gave me no real satisfaction. I was restless, and for some time had had a strong feeling that there was something else I ought to be doing. Sue assured me she could handle the business if I came in for one day a week. She was already responsible for everything except the repairs side, which was my pigeon. Someone else could take that on.

We agreed to try it for a year. If I turned out to be no good as a healer I'd go back to the garage.

Word soon got around that there was a healer at Roundstreet Common and people began to come for treatment. But it was building up only slowly. A friend acting on my behalf persuaded me to let her book the town hall in Horsham so that I could give a talk on healing and she advertised it in the local paper. I'd never spoken in public before and I found the 'lecture' part very difficult. It all became much easier when we moved on to 'questions' and I began to get some feedback from my audience. Even years later new patients often told me they had been to that lecture.

My family were growing up fast, and still increasing. Jeremy, my eldest son, was twenty-five and Teresa, my eldest daughter, was twenty-three. Of my five other children Phillip, the eldest, had already reached the age of sixteen. That meant he was eligible to ride a motor-cycle. He had changed after his accident at the age of nine. He had missed out on much of his education and it had been necessary to send him to special schools. He was due to visit an educational assessment centre at Epsom in September of 1977 to find out what kind of work he might be best suited for. Meanwhile, he had a two-stroke 50cc motor-cycle which enabled him to go every day to Billingshurst where he had a temporary job.

As soon as he had passed his seventeenth birthday he began asking me if he could have a more powerful motor-bike, a 250cc machine instead of his 50cc one. I have always regarded motor-bikes as very dangerous machines and at first I resisted. I tried to persuade him to wait till he was eighteen and old enough to drive a car. But Phillip persisted and in the end I gave way. The boy had not had an easy time and this motor-cycle would be an asset to him in his job.

The new machine came on a Friday in August. Phillip was delighted with it — *'Fan-tastic!'* He wasted no time in trying it out.

The next day, Saturday, I was at the Gatwick garage with Sue. A message came through from the police. Phillip had had an accident. He had been taken to Guildford Hospital.

This time the doctors were optimistic. Phillip's leg had been broken and was in traction. There was some internal damage and his spleen would have to be removed. But his head had been protected by the helmet and there was no brain damage. When his mother and I got there he was sitting up in bed, fully conscious and reasonably comfortable. He was more concerned about the state of his motor-bike than about himself; he wanted to know how soon it could be got back on the road.

The police were mystified as to the cause of the accident. Phillip had come off his bike for no apparent reason and had hit two other cars before fetching up at the side of the road. There were no skid marks and the witnesses were baffled as to why he had crashed. No one else was hurt.

During the next six days he was in hospital I of course saw him frequently. There was no real cause for concern, the doctors said. He was recovering well. The only thing that worried me was that he kept on about that motor-bike. Could it be repaired? When could he get it back on the road again?

I said: 'It was a good thing, wasn't it, Phillip, that no one else was hurt in that accident?'

He looked at me for a moment, then said: 'Dad, let's talk about a car.'

The bike was never mentioned again.

Six days after the accident, Friday again, the phone rang late at night. It was the hospital. Suddenly and inexplicably Phillip had died.

This book is about healing, not clairvoyance or spiritualism or other aspects of the paranormal. But the story of Phillip has been of help to so many of my patients that I am going to tell it here briefly. Some readers may find it hard to believe, but I am only setting down what actually happened as I and Sue experienced it.

The news of Phillip's death was all the more of a shock for being unexpected. There was no sleep for us that night. The following morning we three were together at Roundstreet – myself and Sue and Ann, Phillip's mother.

The hospital telephoned to ask if we'd come over to collect Phillip's effects. Neither Ann nor I could face it; the route led past the place where his accident had occurred. I asked Sue if she would go. Unlike us she had only the vaguest idea where Phillip had crashed.

It was a wet, rainy day. Driving back from the hospital, on the A281 just before the B2133 turns off it, she saw a lad standing at the side of the road. She began to slow, thinking he was hoping for a lift. When she got nearer she saw that he was staring as if puzzled at the road. As she went past he looked up. The face was Phillip's. She slowed and stopped. When she looked back the roadside was deserted, the figure had vanished.

Back at Roundstreet she questioned me about the location of the accident. It was exactly where she had seen Phillip. I checked all the details of her description, even to the electric transformer which she had seen at the spot and which up till then I had not noticed. Her story held good. We agreed to keep this extraordinary experience to ourselves, to tell nobody.

The fact that Sue had seen Phillip, or the etheric form of Phillip, tallied with my own conviction that a person's spirit is not extinguished by physical death. By September I had a strong desire to try and make some kind of contact with Phillip, wherever he was now. Friends advised me to go to see Jessie Nason, a sensitive with a gift for making contact with people who have died.

I will always remember the day I went to her flat in London. It was 13 October 1977. She was an affable, cheerful woman who proceeded to talk about the weather. She did not ask me why I had come to see her and I did not volunteer any information.

Suddenly, in the middle of a chat about everyday things, she stopped dead and gave me an odd look.

'Who is that young man standing beside you? No, don't tell me, he's your son.'

There followed a long conversation, which I will not repeat, with Jessie Nason acting as mouthpiece for Phillip. I could see no one else in the room. But she reproduced Phillip's exact intonation and phraseology and told me a lot of personal and trivial things about him. Some of these I was only able to verify when I got back home, but all were true. I was being told all these things, she said, to prove that I really was in touch with Phillip.

Much of what she said was very comforting to me. Phillip had shown her a road, Jessie said, and told her that he had died in hospital. It would not have happened unless he had insisted on something and I was not to blame myself. He'd been supposed to go when he was nine but had been given a second chance.

He also said, Jessie told me, that Sue had seen him since he'd died. I knew that neither Sue nor I had mentioned this to a living soul.

Here was a complete stranger telling me about matters which were only known inside my most intimate family circle. But what I found most comforting was the impression I had of Phillip's happiness and contentment. Whatever state he was in now it was *fan-tastic!*

In the car outside I made careful notes while my memory was fresh. I intended to check every detail to see if I could fault Jessie Nason. I drove home with feelings of great peace and gratitude.

That was not the end of it. All the checking of details simply confirmed what Jessie had said. The best way I could think of expressing my gratitude was to ask her down to spend a day in the country with us. It was some months before she was able to take me up on my offer.

We walked round the garden and then went indoors for some tea. We were all sitting talking when she said: 'Your boy is with us now. He's standing over there by the fireplace.'

Again she relayed a piece of information which was totally unexpected. 'Your eldest daughter is moving house.'

'No, she's not,' I said. Teresa lived thirty miles away and we were daily ringing each other up.

'Oh, but she is,' Jessie insisted. 'That's what Phillip's telling me.'

To settle the matter I went to telephone my daughter.

'Yes, Dad, we are moving house.'

'But why haven't you mentioned it?'

'We didn't want to tell anyone until the contracts were exchanged. We only exchanged today.'

When Jessie had gone Sue told me that she too had seen Phillip. Just his face and then only for a moment before it faded.

It was not the face of the boy who had suffered brain damage, with its slightly bland expression, but Phillip as he *would* have been at the age of seventeen if the tractor had not run over him when he was nine.

After that I did not persist in trying to make contact with Phillip. I don't think one should combat bereavement in this way. One must turn to those still living in this world with an open and giving attitude. It is enough to know that there is a bond of love which is not broken by death.

Startling results

Phillip's accident and what happened in its aftermath inevitably took much of my attention away from healing. But patients continued to come and I was able to help most of them, some with startling results. During the autumn and winter the flow increased and it was beginning to look as if my experimental year away from the garage business was going to be justified.

One of my patients during that first year was Sue Beasley, a seventeen-year-old girl who had been accidentally shot in the right knee by a twelve-bore shotgun at a range of six feet. She was in constant acute pain. X-rays showed that much of the joint had been blown away and there were shot pellets lodged in her flesh. An operation to render the knee-joint rigid was considered, even amputation was a possibility. She held out against both of these drastic options. Her mother spoke to me on the telephone and I offered my help. She brought her daughter to Roundstreet to see what could be done.

Within seconds of the first treatment starting she was free of pain — for the first time in months. She wept, but her tears were of gratitude, relief and that undefinable sense of the loving power which is felt by many who receive healing. She came weekly for treatment over several months. By the end of that time she was able to run, dance and ride a horse or a bicycle. The only trace of the accident was a slightly bent knee, but she was free of pain. X-rays, copies of which are in my possession, now showed that the pellets were still lodged in her flesh. But they also showed something which the doctors could not account for — there had been significant new growth of bone.

I accompanied Sue Beasley when she was examined by an eminent Norwich surgeon in January 1979. In the letter accompanying his report he wrote: 'It is a most interesting case, the really remarkable feature being the relief of pain after the laying on of hands by the Healer in May 1978. I find this very difficult to explain but I enclose a report of the case and some comments which may be of help.'

I am quoting the report in full, suppressing only the surgeon's name and address:

Mr X CBE, SCD, FRCS

24 January 1979

REPORT OF CONSULTATION ON:

MISS SUE BEASLEY, a young lady age 18

The Healer, Mr Edwardes, concerned in this case was previously a garage man and came with the patient. He appeared to be very modest and made no extravagant claims, and was a big, pleasant personality, very articulate, but was not particularly religious and could not explain his gift of healing, except by stating that, when he put his hand on an injured or diseased part of a patient, he did not carry out any manipulation at all and, in fact, he did not actually need to touch the part but just place his hands near and then he felt a force travel through him and through his hands into the patient.

In this particular case, the girl was relieved of her pain which had been very severe, and then gradually recovery of movement and strength occurred.

CLINICAL EXAMINATION 22.1.79

Symptoms:

The patient stated quite definitely that since the first laying on of hands in May 1978, she could walk about one mile without any aids and then got tired, and the knee ached if she did too much on it. She could ride a horse, or a bicycle, and she worked in a general office.

Both knees had been injured by the discharge of a shotgun from in front of the patient, at a distance of about six feet; on the left side it had only injured the thigh muscles but on the right side it destroyed the medial compartment of the knee joint: on examination the left knee-joint was in fact intact, the wound being above the joint on the medial side, mainly over the vastus medialis muscle.

The right knee was in a moderate degree of varus deformity with creaking on movement and some pain on movement and the range of movement was 165° to 65°.

The X-ray of 22 January 1979 showed that the medial compartment of the right knee had been grossly damaged, the articular surface of both the tibia and the femur had been lost and some collapse had taken place, causing the varus deformity. The lateral compartment of the right knee appeared to be intact, with a good cartilage space.

Comments:
This is a case of remarkable and unexplainable relief of pain, after the laying on of hands of Mr Edwardes in May 1978 after a very severe injury to the right knee in November 1976.

The recovery is so good now that one has to advise leaving it alone for the present at any rate.

The varus deformity however would be best corrected by an osteotomy to put the knee in slight valgus, as this would transfer the weight from the damaged medial side of the joint to the intact lateral side. This would make the knee last longer, but one hesitates to do it, when the complaints are so minimal. If the knee is left in varus it will deteriorate more rapidly than if it is changed to a valgus position. The X-ray shows so much disruption that deterioration is inevitable but may be very slow, and some operative procedure, perhaps an arthrodesis or even an artificial knee-joint, may be required later on.

I should, therefore, advise that this patient is kept under very careful observation both clinically and radiologically and I would certainly advise a reassessment in a year's time or before if her symptoms become more troublesome.

In fact, at the time of writing, Sue has not suffered any deterioration. She has not needed an operation or a new knee-joint and is still pursuing all her old activities.

Another patient, who came as a result of my lecture in Horsham, was Mrs Molly Morgan. She had suffered from migraines most of her life and had tried every known cure. I did not discover till later that she'd also had back trouble. Her migraines were cured after the second session and never recurred. She came back later to have healing for an injured arm. In the course of these treatments her back was also healed, though healing had only been sought for her arm.

Molly was amazed by the effectiveness of the healing. She talked about it to her close friend who was a woman doctor in General Practice at Storrington.

That was how I came to meet Dr Priscilla Noble-Mathews. She was so impressed by what she had heard that she came to see me. We had a number of long discussions about healing and my approach to it. She was a Roman Catholic and we did not always see eye to eye on religious matters. I was delighted though that a member of her profession had such an open mind about healing. So often doctors are scornful of what we healers do. Their training makes it difficult for them to accept anything which cannot be explained scientifically, and they are sceptical of cures which are not proven by weighty (and very expensive) medical evidence. Dr Noble-Mathews believed that healing could be complementary to orthodox medicine, which she thought was in danger of losing its way in a maze of chemical drugs; too often overworked doctors were prescribing antibiotics when what the patient needed was to be given a chance to talk and to be listened to.

Her view of the role of a healer was more limited than mine, but I was both surprised and pleased when she agreed to undertake some joint research with me. I am all for closer links between healers and the medical profession. We are all working to the same end and for too long the contribution that Healing can make has been ignored by the medical establishment.

The idea was that the doctor would be able to see patients before healing started and could check the effectiveness of the cure by scientific medical methods. Of course this could only be done with great discretion and only in the case of patients who were willing to cooperate in this kind of research. Many who are healed take the attitude: '*I* know I am better and that's good enough for me; I don't need an X-ray photograph to prove that I am having no more pain.' All the same, it would help to advance scientific knowledge and be of benefit to all if the effectiveness of healing could be proved to the medical profession.

Then they might make more use of healers to complement their own often wonderful work. Orthodox medicine tends to treat only the body whereas healing embraces the whole person.

Our joint research project had the blessing of the KIB (Koestler, Inglis, Bloomfield) Foundation,* which adopted it as one of their approved projects. The KIB Foundation exists to promote research into unorthodox approaches to the relief of disease or illness. It does not itself dispose of funds but is registered as a charity, so that any donations or bequests channelled through it can benefit from the tax concessions available to administrators of a charitable trust. The kind of research that Dr Noble-Mathews had in mind would involve considerable expense (bear in mind that in 1982 the National Health Service cost about £225 a year from every man, woman and child in the country) and could only go ahead if funds became available. However, as I always have great hopes that things will sort themselves out if you give the Guv'nor a chance, I was ready to go ahead. The KIB had at their disposal a panel of advisors and one of them was Dr Richard Tonkin, a Fellow of the Royal College of Physicians. He came down to Roundstreet to talk to Priscilla and me and advise us on how to set the research up. The KIB brochure described the Roundstreet Project as 'a longitudinal study of the effects of hand-healing'.

A practical problem was accommodation. To begin with I had done my healing in the old Tudor part of the main house. A flight of steps led up from my study to a small room or landing under the eaves and I used this as a healing-room. It was far from ideal. Some patients could not manage the stairs and I was very much on top of the life of the house. There was certainly no room for the doctor to interview and examine patients.

Opposite the front door of the house was the coach-house, which I'd had my eye on for some time. I was sure it could be adapted to provide a waiting-room and a healing-room for me plus a small office and surgery for the doctor. The improvements and refurbishing would cost a bit of money, so I made an appointment to see my bank manager.

He received me in his private office, very friendly and affable till I told him that I wanted to borrow £3,000 — then his eyebrows went up.

'Well, I'm not sure that we can help you there, Mr Edwardes.'

*Now renamed The Koestler Foundation.

'But I've been a customer of yours for fifteen years and you've lent me money before.'

'Yes, I appreciate that, but things were different then. You don't have a regular job any more, do you?'

'No'.

'What security can you offer?'

'None, I'm afraid. That's why I need the loan.'

He pursed his lips and looked very dubious. It so happened that I had in my briefcase a copy of *Psychic News.* In it was an article about some of my patients and how they had been healed. On an impulse I took it out and handed it to him, folded at the place.

He put on his glasses and read it through. Then he looked at me thoughtfully.

'Do you know, I once went to a healer. His name was Harry Edwards. He had a place near Guildford. I had trouble with my hip and the doctors were getting nowhere with it. But Harry Edwards healed it. I've never had any trouble with it since.'

I said: 'Perhaps you can see from that article that I work for the Guv'nor too.'

'Yes,' he agreed with a smile. 'I think you do.'

'Well, where,' I asked him, 'where could you get a better reference for a loan?'

With the bank's £3,000 behind me I was able to put the necessary alterations in hand straightaway.

All of these developments were spread over quite a long period of time, during which my family continued to grow. Sue, who had already given me two sons, was expecting a third baby. In addition to raising a family she was also still supervising the garage at Gatwick. I had now completely severed my connection with that operation in order to devote all my available time to healing, but we still needed the income from the garage to live on.

There was now a pretty constant stream of people coming to Roundstreet for healing. Some of these had been sent to me by Dr Noble-Mathews. The doctor did not tell me anything about her patients except their name. She left me to find out their problems.

One of these was a woman who had been stone deaf from birth. Even a hearing-aid was no good to her. She had the sing-song voice of those who have never been able to hear themselves speak, but she was adept at lip-reading and could understand what I said. I naturally assumed she had come about her deafness but no, it was her rheumatoid arthritis she wanted help with. She had it in her shoulders, knees and hands. I gave her healing for both ailments and she came to me fifteen times during the next three months.

Now, before she first came to me her GP had sent blood samples to the medical laboratory for testing. The report came back with a recommendation that she should be given gold injections — a drastic remedy. Her doctor knew that she was coming to me for healing and that her rheumatoid arthritis was improving; so she played for time and deferred a decision about the gold injections.

After two months and six visits she was so much better that her GP took another lot of blood samples and sent them off to the laboratory. The report that came back stated that the gold injections were no longer necessary. A month later she was able to go back to work.

That is not the end of her story. She had never considered the possibility that she might gain the power to hear. She had only asked for her rheumatoid arthritis to be eased. But she was receptive to healing and healing was strong for her.

During the treatment she became aware that she was beginning to hear. The improvement was apparent from her second visit. By the fifth she was feeling better in her whole self and had begun to hear with a transistor hearing-aid. On her eighth visit she felt the healing power even before I started. I was treating her sinuses that day and she later told me that her sense of smell as well as her hearing had both improved.

I was a little impatient with the slow improvement in her hearing and was doing my best to speed it up. The result showed me that it is best to leave everything in the hands of the Guv'nor. She told me one day that during a brief spell of improved hearing she had heard a motor-bike passing by. And the sound *hurt.* I realized then that it would be painful for a person deaf from birth to gain the sense of hearing too rapidly. The gift had to be given gradually.

There is always something new to be learned and this experience reminded me of the kindly intelligence behind all healing. I was prepared to continue treating her with much greater patience over a long period. Then abruptly, after twelve visits and with no explanation, she stopped coming to me. Only much later did I discover the reason for this and it was *not* because the healing was proving ineffective.

Another patient Dr Noble-Mathews passed on to me was in her middle forties. She had been suffering from depression on and off for seventeen years. These bouts of depression were severe enough to prevent her from eating or sleeping. When I gave her healing I did not feel that it was very strong, but she felt it very strongly, even to the point of OBE. (OBE or Out of Body Experience is when people feel as if their mind has become detached from their body; often they seem to be looking back at their physical body from some distance away.) She came back for treatment at intervals of four days, five days and eleven days. Then she stayed away for two months. When she came back at the end of July she told me that she was getting a full night's sleep. She was no longer using sleeping pills and her depression had gone. My last note on her says: 'Feels she is healed and so do I'.

Joanne was much younger, only seventeen years old. She was a sufferer from hay fever, and had a chest infection. From childhood her sleep had been disturbed and this had robbed her of energy. She had one healing session. That evening her nose and eyes absolutely streamed. She spent the next day in a field behind a combine harvester without any sign of hay fever. Her sense of smell, her ability to take a proper night's sleep and above all her energy were restored from that day — 21 August.

Such examples of rapid betterment are more frequent in the young. Older people have problems which are less easily remedied. One is bereavement.

Bereavement may cause intense depression and though this is a mental condition it can cause harm to the physical body. Healing, though, is for the whole person — the mind and spirit as well as the body. Dr Noble-Mathews sent me a patient who was very low following the loss of her husband. When I say 'low' I mean she was in black despair, unable to face life or take part in anything. On her first visit we talked for two hours before I gave her healing. But it was the talk that did the real healing and I had guidance about what to say. On her second visit twelve days later the talk lasted for just one hour. By then she was already taking part in life again. Since then I have had no contact with her.

Meanwhile, repairs to the outbuilding were going ahead. I was doing the work myself, laying bricks, building a chimney stack of which I am not very proud, fixing guttering, putting a pine ceiling in the healing-room. Sue had already given birth to her third son and was still having to do her job at the garage. Without her pay we had not enough to live on.

'Don't worry,' we'd been told. 'Sue will be at home before the baby is toddling.'

Amongst her many activities at the garage, Sue always organized a little syndicate of eight that put in an entry every week for Littlewood's Football Pool. One day in September she was sitting at her desk which commanded a view of the forecourt. She saw a man park his car and get out. He was wearing a business suit and carrying a briefcase. She thought he looked just like the kind of official who comes round to inspect the toilet facilities or the VAT records, so when he came into her office she received him warily.

'You are Susan Edwardes of Salford's Garage, Gatwick?'

'That's right.'

'I've come to inform you that you have won the top prize in Littlewood's Football Pool.'

It was obviously some sort of spoof, so Sue kept up the game.

'Oh, yes. How much for?'

'£750,000.'

It took him all of five minutes to convince her that this was no joke. *We had won the Pools!*

Of course, the prize had to be divided into eight, the number of people in the syndicate. Legally, as only her name was on the entry, Sue could have taken the lot. One of the eight was a girl who had actually left her job at the garage the previous week. Sue had paid her ante for her and included her in the syndicate this one last time. Even the girl did not know that she was 'in', but Sue, typically, insisted that she must have her share. It came to £93,750 each.

We had to go up to London for the ceremonial presentation of the enormous cheque by Littlewood's, though it was actually handed over to us by the comedians Little and Large. The photographers were more interested in the celebrated comics than in the eight grinning winners from Salford's Garage.

There were lots of lads there from the City to tell us how to invest our money. Tony Bloomfield of KIB had already rung up to advise me: 'Don't accept anything less than 17 per cent.' That made me a little wary of the representative of a well-known High Street bank who came to Roundstreet and told me that as a special gesture he could get me 8 per cent.

This windfall made all the difference to us. With the income from our capital we had enough to live on. Sue was able to give up her job at the garage and be at home all the time – just as Toby started toddling.

Most satisfactory of all, I was able to repay the loan the bank manager had granted me and prove to him that his confidence in my credit-worthiness had not been misplaced.

The flow of patients

There had been no doubt in my mind about what this manna from heaven was to be used for. It provided us with independent means so that I could continue to work as a healer and Sue could fulfil her role as mother and housewife. Being unearned income, the revenue attracted a higher rate of tax. My net income was now at the level of a dustman's.

Just then interest rates were high. When they fell a couple of years later our income was much reduced.

People sometimes judge a healer by the kind of life he leads. Many expect that, because he is exercising a God-given gift, he should adopt a life of penury and self-denial, not only for himself but for his family as well. Contrary to popular belief, a healer is not someone special – he is a human being like anybody else. It is true that the more genuinely caring he is about those who come to him for help, the more effective his healing will be. If he was so self-centred that his aim in life was to amass material possessions it is unlikely that he would be a good healer. Some critics argue that a true healer should make no monetary charge for his services. But a healer has a stomach and so have his family. If he has given up all other means of support it is only fair that he should have something to live on.

I live a simple life with few luxuries but I do not fast or perform arduous religious exercises. I enjoy life and the good things of this earth. If the Guv'nor did not intend us to enjoy his creation why did he make it so beautiful and provide us with the senses to appreciate it? Since I became a healer my life and outlook have of course changed. But I am in no sense an ascetic and am certainly not anyone's idea of a guru or holy man.

A healer needs to have a supportive family, especially a wife who believes in what he is doing and is prepared to make sacrifices for it. I am lucky because my family really do try to back me up. The kids are very good about not making a noise playing round the healing-room and take it philosophically when I am out there with patients until hours after they have gone to bed. Just as she took on all the awkward jobs when we were running the garage together, so Sue now deals with all the chores involved in bringing up a quartet of four lusty boys. That gives me the freedom of mind I need if I am to do my healing job properly. I do, however, keep my weekends free. It enables me to see something of my family and also gives me a chance to relax and build up energy for the next week's healing work.

With Sue at home most of the time I had a much more favourable background for my healing. Work on the coach-house was now completed. For my own use I had an ante-room where I could have my preliminary talk with patients as well as the healing-room beyond it. This was a pleasant room which has always had a good atmosphere. Adjoining my rooms were the two smaller ones which I had prepared and furnished for Dr Noble-Matthews, thanks to the loan from the bank — an office and a little surgery. She was now able to see her private patients there and, in cases where she thought it appropriate, advise them to come to me.

Though it had the moral support of the KIB Foundation the Roundstreet Project still had no funds. The total Sue had won for us on the Pools could in no way have covered the costs of the medical research which it was planned to set up. Besides, without the income from our windfall I would not have been able to continue as a healer. I considered it important to do so. No elaborate research was needed to prove to me that healing was effective. I *knew* that it worked. Healing comes a good deal cheaper than orthodox medicine. The Guv'nor needs no props, just the workaday body and hands of your humble servant.

We did not attract the attention of any benefactor, but we did rouse the interest of the media. During 1980-1 Anglia Television were preparing a documentary series of films on what is sometimes referred to as alternative medicine. The title of the series was *The Medicine Men,* and there was also to be a book based on it. (*The Medicine Men* by John Lloyd Fraser, published by Thames/Methuen 1981.) Each of the eight weekly programmes was to feature one of the complementary forms of medicine. Healing was fifth on the list.

The television people were particularly interested in the

co-operation between the 'former garage owner' and a local General Practitioner. Both the doctor and I made ourselves available to the TV crew who came down for a day's filming at Roundstreet. The series was shown in the early months of 1982 and our reward was a brief shot of me in the healing room with one of my patients.

The showing of this film had good results. A number of patients who came to me subsequently said that seeing *The Medicine Men* or reading the book had made them decide to give healing a try.

It was a great pity when soon after this Dr Noble-Mathews moved away to another practice outside the area. I did not give up hope that the kind of collaboration she and I had started would in the course of time be continued, and that hope now looks like being justified.

I still had plenty of work on my hands, for the flow of patients was steadily increasing. The people who came or were brought to see me had nothing in common except that they were all ailing in one way or another. There was tremendous variation in the type of illness for which they were seeking help, and also in their attitudes towards healing. Almost without exception they were cases where orthodox medicine had failed. Many had already tried other forms of complementary medicine – homoeopathy, hypnotism or acupuncture.

They had come to me as a last resort.

In the nature of things they tended to be fairly desperate by the time they came to my door. Most had no previous experience of healing and in the first place were wary, fearful or even sceptical about what might be going to happen.

Healing in many people's minds was associated with the 'occult' and that word conjured up all sorts of inhibitions. Again, it was usual for new patients to feel that some big effort would be required on their part in terms of belief or faith. An elderly woman who came was the niece of a famous Archbishop of Canterbury. She asked me on her first visit: 'Do I have to have faith?' I told her she needn't, and she said: 'Thank God, 'cos I haven't got any!' As it turned out, healing for her was very strong.

Oddly enough it is religious people rather than agnostics who have difficulty in accepting healing. Members of established Churches often come with a sense of guilt, feeling that by going to a lay healer they are being unfaithful to their own ministers. There might be a slightly guilty feeling for another reason; only in rare cases have my patients told their doctor what they were doing.

In a number of ways my capacity as a healer has increased over the years, because as I went on I learned more and more about it. I had no textbook to guide me. Each healer works in his own particular way and he has to find out how he can get the best results. He also comes to know himself better; he learns how to compensate for his weaknesses and exploit his strengths. Though I have seen perhaps two thousand patients each individual is different and so there can be no set rules. There is always something new to learn.

The case of Angela S was a good example of the way healing can eradicate a most complex pattern of disease. Angela had suffered pain in various parts of her body for years. It stemmed from a number of causes. She'd had a smallpox vaccination as long ago as 1962 and her reaction was so bad that she became prone to recurring attacks of loss of balance. During her first pregnancy in 1968 she began to feel pain in her right arm and numbness in the fingers of her right hand. The same thing happened during her second pregnancy. Then she developed a slipped disc and in 1978 went down with an attack of glandular fever. She now had severe pain in the neck and head. X-rays indicated that the cause of this was a closing up of the vertebrae in her neck. Her sight was impaired and the loss of balance became steadily worse. By the following year she was experiencing tinnitus (ringing in the ears), and tests showed some loss of hearing. Her condition was diagnosed as Menière's disease. Orthodox medicine seemed unable to alleviate this variety of unpleasant symptoms so, as a last resort, she decided to come to me. She visited me almost every week from November 1980 until April 1981. Healing was gradual but steady and by the end of the treatment she was cured, free of pain and discomfort.

Phyllis A, a nurse, was suffering from nephritis and osteoarthritis in her upper back and knees. Her first response to healing was immediate and dramatic and thereafter she made steady improvement. After eleven visits she was completely all right.

Edward J was cured with amazing rapidity. When he came

to me he was awaiting an operation for hernia. During his second healing session he felt a contraction in his stomach and afterwards all the symptoms of hernia disappeared. His doctor was able to confirm that the operation was no longer necessary. Not long afterwards he was involved in a car accident and had pain in his shoulder and spine. This was put right in one healing session.

His wife had for years been suffering from painful osteoarthritis, so she decided to try healing also. Often I am left with no idea of how successful or otherwise my efforts have been. Sensing, perhaps, that the healing comes not from me but from beyond me some patients are reticent about their experience and prefer to keep such things in their heart. Others vanish and I have no way of telling whether the healing cured them completely or they'd decided it was a complete flop. Mrs J however was kind enough to write to me later:

> When I came to you I had suffered many years of pain. After my first session the pain disappeared completely from my spine and when I walked out I realized it had also gone from my foot. The pain in my neck lessened each day until it had disappeared completely by the fourth day. The pain in my right shoulder is still persistent, but even so it is wonderful to feel so much better.
>
> What is fresh in my mind is a feeling of being completely relaxed with a coolness down my spine and a sense of tranquillity and peacefulness. I also see colours (during healing) and on my first visit with my eyes closed I saw both beautiful colours and fast-moving landscapes. On a subsequent visit I saw a sort of kaleidoscope of coloured jewels, very vivid, and with purple fish all swimming in a whirlpool.

Jenny M, whom I treated for eye trouble and a painful back, wrote to describe a similar experience:

> At the time of the healing session I saw flames rising up from the bottom of my vision to about half-way, where they would disappear and re-start at the bottom. Sometimes my whole vision would be like looking into a furnace. When you (Phil) placed your hands on my forehead my vision blacked out.

During the whole of the journey home in the car she felt extremely light-headed and her shoulders were 'alive with a constant surge of energy'. That evening she started to feel extremely tired.

> It was then that I realized that my eye had not given me any pain during the drive home, whereas it had given me a lot of pain during the journey over. Since, I noticed my left eye dribbling continuously but feeling much stronger. At night the pain has been much less, more subdued. My back has given me no pain since the healing session.

One Monday evening I received a telephone call from Coral Atkins, the actress. Her mother, who had been a good friend to me since my Newbury days, had been involved in a car accident. She had been thrown out of her own car on to the road, and the other car in the accident had driven over her pelvis. This was particularly serious because Lily was an elderly woman. Coral told me that she had been taken to Battle Hospital, Reading and asked if I could help. Unfortunately my healing commitments at Roundstreet prevented me from visiting her until the following Thursday. In the meantime I did what I could by means of distant healing.

When I eventually was able to visit the hospital Coral told me that her mother had recovered well from the shock but she had multiple injuries and her pelvis was broken in five places. I found Lily in bed in a general ward which was full of the usual bustle and movement of people. It was a sunny day, warm but not unpleasantly hot. Coral was accompanied by an actor-producer boyfriend of hers and by her younger sister.

Lily had about twenty stitches in the back of one hand. Her head and one foot had been stitched up and bandaged. Her left side from the knee to the waist had been left exposed to the air and not dressed. She had been dragged along the road during the accident and the whole of this area was skinned and bruised. The wound was open and raw and the bruising was a spectacular blend of blue, green and yellow. The bedclothes were still turned back from this huge raw patch.

Lily stretched her hands towards me. I took them in both of mine and concentrated hard as I tried to give her healing in this busy ward. After a time I began to feel very hot, the sweat poured off me. I glanced round to see if anyone else was feeling such heat, but they were all quite normal, looking down at Lily.

Then Coral's friend exclaimed: 'My God, look at that!'

Everyone stared at the thigh wound. It had suddenly changed in appearance. The bruising had disappeared and a scab was beginning to form over the wound, which had been open and raw. During that brief session while I was holding Lily's hands it had healed up as much as you would expect in a normal fortnight.

The great intelligence behind healing knew that the first priority was to heal this wound. One of the most important factors in a case such as Lily's is shock, exacerbated by pain. Her pelvis had been made comfortable, she could not see the injury on her head, and her hand and foot were covered in bandages. But she could see and feel the ghastly wound on her leg. That is why it was dealt with first of all, and speedily too.

I went to see her after her discharge from hospital. Despite her age she was back to normal and able to move about freely. She told me that her recovery had started 'from the healing hands you gave me'. She also said that at the time my hands were holding hers she was praying for me!

Incidentally, the actor-manager was so impressed by what he had seen that he rang up to ask if he could bring his own mother to me for healing. 'I thought you'd like to know,' he said, 'that after you left the hospital the other day I went back to the ward to make sure I hadn't been seeing things! I satisfied myself that Lily's leg really had changed.'

By praying during her healing Lily really had helped because she was providing the best conditions for the healing power to flow. Such a positive open attitude, whether intentionally prayerful or not, does seem to enhance the effectiveness of healing, whereas a negative attitude may inhibit it. Formal religious belief however is *not* necessary. An agnostic who comes with an open mind is more likely to be made well than a churchy person who has a sense of guilt because he feels he is dabbling in the paranormal.

Guilt is not the only emotion to form a barrier. Fear can be an equally strong inhibitor. The cases of two women who both came to me because they had cancer make it tragically clear that attitudes of mind may make all the difference between life and death.

The first, aged about fifty, had cancer of the lung. She confided to me that her doctor had told her, in a very casual manner: 'You won't live until the spring.' The district nurse, making one of her regular visits, had asked whether she wanted to die at home or in hospital! Between them they had managed to convince her that her illness was hopeless. By the time she came to me she was utterly terrified.

I did my best to encourage a positive attitude in her by insisting that the doctor and the nurse were not necessarily right and that she could be cured by healing. Unfortunately her outlook was locked in fear and hopelessness and I could not change it. Although she experienced some relief during treatment she died at Christmas time.

In marked contrast was another woman of about the same age. She was the wife of a local coal merchant and she too had cancer. There was a large painful lump on her breast just below her shoulder and she had difficulty in swallowing. Now, she had previously been healed of a spinal complaint, so she had the confidence to place herself entirely in my hands.

'I neither know nor care about medical treatment,' she said. 'I'm sure I can be healed just as well by you here as in hospital.'

She visited me twice weekly from November 1980 till February 1981 and thereafter once a week. To start with the pain in her breast lessened, then the lump softened and began to shrink till it finally disappeared. Her throat improved so that she could swallow without pain. Her digestion, which had been bad, gradually improved. All in all she improved so much generally that she believed she was cured. But I persuaded her to continue with the regular treatment until I was convinced that her recovery was complete. She is still coming to me and there is no doubt in my mind that one day she will be completely clear. I just know it.

Knowledge of that kind plays an important part in healing. The Guv'nor has ways of guiding the healer when patients have unusually difficult problems.

My daughter Teresa persuaded a friend of hers to come and see me. This girl was having to go regularly to a mental hospital for treatment. She kept hearing 'voices'. At the mental hospital they had told her it was just her imagination. We had our usual preliminary talk. She told me about these 'voices' which kept plaguing her, nagging her, telling her to do this, that or the other.

I sought guidance as I often do in such cases. I heard someone say: 'Not voices. One voice.'

I said to my patient: 'You don't really mean voices, do you? It's one voice. The voice of one person.'

She looked at me, startled. Yes, she agreed, it was one voice.

What transpired was that this was the voice of an extremely tiresome woman who had lived in the house next door and had passed on. I told her how to deal with it and a little later she phoned me to say that the voice had been stilled. She never had to go to the mental hospital again.

Such cases are normally dealt with by a psychiatrist. The treatment generally consists of drugs. In fact, psychiatrists prescribe more drugs than any other kind of specialist. I have had no training in psychotherapy — nor indeed in any other branch of medicine. But I know that the healing required for disturbances of the mind is different. Often it may consist of just talking to the patient. And this is where I am helped. I seem to be told what to say.

Many come to me with severe depression. It may be because of bereavement or it may have other causes. Depression can have serious consequences. It may be there without any apparent cause. A man came to me once whose life was in ruins because of this. He had suffered severe bouts since childhood and had now reached the point where he could not come out of his depression. His despair and hatred of the world had made him violent towards himself, his family, even the dog. His wife had left him and he had lost his job. At his mother's instigation he came to me regularly over a period of two months. The healing took mostly the form of talking — sometimes this is called counselling. It must have been the right treatment because by the end of the healing period he had become a rational human being. His wife went back to him and assured me on the phone how very happy they both were. He got his old job back and his firm were so pleased that they raised his salary to make sure he stayed with them.

Even when healing apparently failed there was often betterment in unexpected ways.

Pam C was a case in point. She was a sufferer from multiple sclerosis and had been in a wheelchair for twenty years. She had pain in the upper part of her body and needed help to sit up straight after she had been leaning back in her chair. Her hands were so deformed that her fingers were fixed in a hooked position. Healing freed her from the pain she had suffered for so long and she became able to sit up without help. Gradually her hands became a little looser. That was the extent of her physical improvement. My hope that I might one day see her walking again was not to be fulfilled.

One day she brought me a painting she had done herself. It was a still-life of flowers and remarkably good. She'd never had an art lesson in her life and considering the state of her hands it was hard to understand how she could even hold a brush. I gave her some roses from my own garden to take home and next time she came she brought me a delicate and beautiful study of them. I still have it hanging in my healing-room.

She told me that she could not stop painting now, she wanted to do it all the time.

Before a year had passed she phoned to tell me that she was still spending most of her time painting. Her work was so successful and popular that she was actually selling pictures.

'I wanted you to know how happy I am,' she said.

The healing had not freed her from her wheelchair, but something else had happened. In the past, as she could not walk, she had been entirely dependent on the good will of other people. Now it was she who could give pleasure to others and this was a real release and fulfilment. So, in terms of the whole person, her case had not been a failure. The awakening of a creative talent had been her form of healing.

It is difficult to judge whether or not one has failed. I would never deny that I personally sometimes fail, but I would hesitate to say that healing had failed. I have emphasized already that it is not I who does the healing. The help of the loving designer is always available to anyone suffering from disease. If the healing 'fails' it is because for some reason the patient is not able to accept it. Remember that healing is for the whole person – spirit as well as body. The example of Pam C shows that the healing of the spirit can be the greater betterment. Indeed, if the physical disease was cured and the spirit remained untouched I would say that was a failure.

The tragic failures are those who never seek healing at all. Tragic is a word often misused but what could be more tragic than that the great love which expresses itself in healing is available to all, yet many cannot bring themselves to accept it?

There have been times when I knew that I had failed in my approach to a patient. A Hindhead man aged about fifty wrote to me and asked if I would give him healing. He was suffering from lung cancer. When he came we sat down and had the usual talk. I had not got far into my explanation about healing when he put up his hand and stopped me.

'I've looked into all this,' he said angrily, 'and I cannot have anything to do with the kind of healing you practise here.'

He did take the trouble to write to me and explain what I was doing wrong; healing should be performed under the auspices of the Church and accompanied by the prayers of ministers. Naturally I felt that with him I had failed.

I also thought I had failed with a woman who had suffered from a thyroid tumour for fourteen years. She had already been to two well-known healers. There was a lot of healing for her and she felt heat in the thyroid, but there was not immediately any apparent improvement. She came four times then disappeared from my ken. A considerable time later she reappeared with a much younger woman who turned out to be her daughter. She had persuaded the daughter to come to me because I had healed her, the mother. She had not come back herself because her thyroid tumour had been cured. I suppose she thought I would know about this instinctively.

Sometimes patients think that healing has failed when I know that it has succeeded. A woman who had curvature of the spine maintained that there was no improvement from visit to visit. To convince her I had to put measuring marks on the wall to show her how, centimetre by centimetre, her spine was straightening and she was able to stand more erect.

The angry man I mentioned earlier was not the only one who was uneasy because I do not have religious symbols about the place. It is hard for some people to accept that a healer can work outside the framework of any Church. One good lady confided to me that she had expected to find a large hall full of people and myself standing up on a platform, with all of us singing hymns before the healing commenced. Another who felt too worldly to qualify for healing said to me rather shyly: 'My Dad did once belong to the Salvation Army, is that all right?'

It is not always practicable for me to make an accurate assessment of how effective healing has been. People come to me of their own free will and nothing obliges them to return.

There are even those who have reasons for not wanting to be healed.

An example was the woman who had been deaf from birth and to whom the gift of hearing was being given through healing. At the end of three months she had reached the stage where she could hear a motor-cycle passing in the street. Abruptly she stopped attending for treatment. It was not a question of money for she had not been in a position to pay anything even if she had wanted to. I knew that her husband was stone deaf, but he had never wanted healing for himself. Their friends were all folk who suffered from the same affliction. He had warned her by sign language: 'If you get your healing you will be different from us.' I came to the conclusion that she feared if she ceased to be deaf it would cause problems in their relationship, so she decided not to take the risk.

An employee of the Post Office had received a serious injury at work and suffered brain danage. His speech was badly affected. When he came to me approximately one word in six was comprehensible. There was healing for him but he went away without saying much. That evening he phoned me and we were able to have an almost normal conversation. Nineteen words out of twenty were now comprehensible. This seemed to have been a rapid and effective betterment. Yet he did not go on with the treatment. And the reason? His wife had been making great efforts to establish a claim for compensation against his employers. If his speech had been restored to normal it would have affected their chances of a financial settlement.

Fervent Christian beliefs of a certain kind may come between a person and effective healing. I had a patient aged about sixty-seven who was a staunch Methodist. She had osteoarthritis in both hips and also suffered from circulatory trouble. An operation had been performed to insert a steel pin in her hip. As a result, her right leg was a quarter of an inch shorter than the left and she had to wear a built-up shoe. A second operation on the other hip was really required but this was considered inadvisable because of her general state of health. There was healing for her and the first sign was that the built-up shoe became uncomfortable to wear. Then, sitting in the bath one day, she noticed that her legs were of equal length. This was subsequently confirmed by her doctor and the built-up shoe was discarded.

I was surprised by this. My own thoughts had been directed to the arthritic hip and not the shorter leg. Once again I had confirmation that a better intelligence than mine was at work. Now I understand that before the hip could be put right it was necessary for the legs to become of equal length and the hips aligned so as to avoid strain on the joint.

This patient was constantly drawing me into discussion on my religious beliefs, which the reader will realize are not exactly orthodox. I answered her questions as honestly as I could, but it was obvious that our viewpoints were very different.

Then one day she asked me as soon as she arrived not to talk to her during her visits. Under the circumstances the request for silence was a bit odd, and it is hard to give healing to someone if you can't talk to them. Next morning her husband telephoned me. I was not to talk to his wife during healing sessions, and would I kindly give a promise to that effect, because the things I was saying were disturbing her faith. I expressed surprise that such a firmly-established faith could be affected by anything I might say.

She did not attend again, so a course of healing which had been going remarkably well had to be abandoned.

I learned the sequel to this from another patient who was a member of the same Methodist Church. A visiting minister had been talking at a church meeting and had got onto the subject of healing. My erstwhile patient rose to confess that she had been to a non-Methodist healer. He had tried to take her away from Christ, she said, so she had ceased to go to him. The minister confirmed that she had done the right thing. Any healer who was not a Methodist, he added, was working for the Devil.

All too often this is the attitude of Church leaders. They acknowledge that healing can happen and they call it Faith Healing. But they insist that it should be done under the auspices of the Church, otherwise it is to be regarded with suspicion if not downright condemnation. This gives the unfortunate impression that God only cares about church members and can only work through church ministers. The Church does not take the same attitude towards the medical profession, whose religious views are not regarded as relevant.

Not all clergy are so limited in their outlook. In fact a Roman Catholic priest aged sixty-seven came to me for healing, complete with dog-collar and black clericals. He opened our discussion by saying: 'I want you to know that I am completely open-minded about this.' He was suffering from advanced cancer of the lung. During his visits we had very lively discussions and came to the conclusion that we were both working for the same Guv'nor.

After four treatments he was much better, and wrote me a charming letter to say so. He was not able to attribute his recovery solely to my efforts, he said, because his entire congregation had been praying for him!

The medical establishment has traditionally been very wary of all kinds of healers. It is right that they should want to protect the public from bogus healers, but all too often when healing really is effective the doctors just don't want to know. They frequently attribute the cure to what is called 'spontaneous remission'.

I know of the case of a woman whose illness was diagnosed as incurable. In desperation she sought help from a healer and he was able to cure her. She went back to her doctor who confirmed that the disease had disappeared. 'You have a spontaneous remission,' he told her.

During the following weeks she became quite ill again, showing all kinds of different symptoms. Then she happened to meet a friend who knew more about medical terminology than she did. The friend explained that 'spontaneous remission' was not some dreadful new illness. From that time on she completely recovered her health.

There is great variation in the attitude of doctors, and patients have no way of knowing how they will react. Many of my patients who have been cured of disease when orthodox medicine has failed do not tell their doctors about it. Not only do they have a guilty feeling that they have gone behind the doctor's back but they are afraid that the doctor will disbelieve or even ridicule the evidence of a cure. Several patients have told their GP or specialist that their remarkable recovery has been due to healing and have been encouraged to continue. The mood in the medical profession is changing. More and more professional doctors are becoming interested in the work of genuine healers. Dr Noble-Mathews is a case in point. I have had patients sent along to me by other doctors. One was so determined that a man suffering pain after the removal of his coccyx should go to a healer that he threatened to remove the patient's name from his panel if he did not do so.

The government has been less tentative than the Church or the medical profession in recognizing healers. 'Healer' now figures in the Department of Employment's list of accredited occupations.

Swami

By the end of 1981 my life had settled into a regular pattern, broken only by the arrival of Sue's fourth son. Timothy was born under the sign of Taurus in that year, bringing my total tally of offspring up to eight.

It was early in 1982 that I had one of the most important experiences of my life. I flew out to India to see Sai Baba.

I had read a lot about this great Indian mystic in *Psychic News.* What I had learned filled me with wonder and incredulity. Several of the articles were by Peggy Mason and Ron Laing. I phoned them and they invited me over to see them. To tell the truth I wanted to find out if they were crackers or not. They impressed me deeply, and I decided that the only thing to do was to go out to India and see for myself.

On 8 January I set off accompanied by my friend Robert, who also has a healing gift. Thanks to the practical advice of Peggy and Ron we were equipped with mosquito net, bed roll, water-purifying tablets, loo paper, etc. We departed from Heathrow in a snowstorm and landed in Bombay thirty hours later to face heat that was like the kitchen oven on a Sunday. We spent a dreadful day waiting for the 'plane on to Bangalore.

Sai Baba has two main *ashrams,* the main one at Puttaparthi, where he was born, and another at Whitefields. Whitefields, a former British-owned estate, is only seventeen miles from Bangalore. No one knows for certain where Sai Baba is going to be, with the possible exception of his elephant, an animal so devoted to him that it will walk a hundred miles to be by his side. Humans will travel further than that. They come from all over the world merely to be in the presence of this extraordinary man.

We booked in at a second-class hotel, the Bangalore International, and soon discovered that we were in luck. Swami, the name by which his followers called Sai Baba, was at Whitefields. Our taxi collected us at 6.30 a.m. the following morning. It was an ancient Morris Oxford Ambassador driven by an engaging Indian who remained in attendance on us all day, eager to help with the shopping, run messages and sit waiting in the merciless sun for hours.

The *ashram* was a vast place with accommodation units, a canteen, student hostel and the Sai Baba University. In the centre is an open space round an ancient baobab tree, where some shelter is provided by a circular shed. Here people wait for Swami's daily appearance, the men segregated from the women. We were among the first but were soon surrounded by a host not only of Indians but Europeans, Asians, North and South Americans and many from the former British Dominions.

What had we come to see? That is another story. Suffice it to say that Sai Baba is not as other men are and that extraordinary things happen in his presence — and ten thousand miles away from him.

He appears twice a day, morning and evening, at what is called *darshan.* A tremendous sense of expectation builds up as the time for his appearance approaches. Then there is a buzz of excitement as a tiny figure emerges from the building and walks to the clear space round the central tree. He is diminutive in size, apparently young, with a head of stiff black hair. He wears a long saffron robe. His smile is beautiful and his presence brings delight.

Strange and inexplicable things happen when he is there. You can read all about them in the books that have been written on Sai Baba. For instance, he throws sweets to the children in the crowd. Where do the sweets come from? He carries no bag. The sweets appear in his hand and fly unerringly into the laps of the children. Sleight of hand?

We'd made friends with a young couple, so in love that they were already on cloud nine. To everyone's surprise a sweet flew into the crowd from Swami and landed on the girl's tummy. Sai Baba was smiling. She was overjoyed. More than nine months had elapsed when I met the couple again. The baby had already been born. She told me that the night before that day at the *ashram* they had made love and she was instantly sure that she had conceived a baby. Swami's sweet greeted it a few hours later.

As Sai Baba slowly moved round, smiling at the crowd, I knew that the moment I had come to India for was approaching. He stopped twelve yards away from where Robert and I were squatting in the crowd.

To my eyes he was surrounded by an aura of brilliant, dazzling light, so bright that he became almost invisible in the middle of it. I was filled with deep emotion and felt impelled to stretch out my hands towards him. It seemed that something passed from him to me, that my hands, often the channel for an outward-flowing power, were now receiving.

He looked at me and I responded like a bell that had been struck. He gazed at me for what seemed an age and I felt that he knew me.

We went back twice a day for the rest of the fortnight. I never spoke with Swami. He was not giving personal interviews at that time. It did not seem to matter. What words spoken or written could have expressed the message that was passed?

Swami's favourite flower is the rose, and it is mine. Months later I was sitting with a group of friends in the healing-room. We were sensitive and open to etheric communication. We felt the level rise to a higher plane than we'd ever known before. A rose fell into my lap. It was not a type that I have in my garden. No one had brought a rose into the room. The door and the window were closed. It was a happening that I cannot begin to explain.

Complementary Medicine

Towards the end of 1982 there were several indications that more members of the medical profession were beginning to become interested in healing.

The first was when a fairly young doctor of psychiatry came to me for healing. He had developed cancer of the stomach. I was sure that it was due to the very stressful nature of his work (at the Tavistock Clinic). We discussed whether he should have the operation that had been offered. I advised him not to refuse such an excellent offer and I suggested that he should have healing before and after it. I was not able to visit him in hospital, but the operation was apparently successful and afterwards he came down several times for healing. My concern was not only to aid his convalescence but to try and help him make a mental adjustment so that he would be less vulnerable to the kind of stress which so often leads to cancer. It was good that healing was being used not as an alternative to orthodox medicine but as a complement to it, and that the patient was himself a qualified doctor.

I also had an interesting enquiry from a consultant neuropsychiatrist at one of London's leading teaching hospitals. He had heard of researches being done in Toronto, Canada, where distilled water which had been 'healed' by a healer showed changes in the infra-red spectrum. I agreed to go up to London to participate in an experiment. Three flasks of twice-distilled water had been prepared. I was asked to apply 'healing' to one of them. This I did in a separate room with one witness. The healing was strong and I had all the usual reactions, including considerable heat in my own body. It lasted for about five minutes. A sample from the flask I had 'healed' was then analysed by a spectrophotometer, a complex machine which draws a line on a sheet of graph paper. Any deviation from the norm would indicate that the distilled water had undergone a change — a totally unexpected result. What the neuropsychiatrist wanted to find out was whether the bonding of the hydrogen and oxygen molecules would be altered. He agreed that if there was such a change it would be very significant. The machine did give a hiccup, but the doctors thought this might be due to a malfunction. The experiment was not completed on that day and at the time of writing there is no conclusive result.

The third development was that Dr Richard Tonkin, whom I mentioned in connection with KIB and the Roundstreet Project, rang me up to say that he was to be chairman of a committee whose task would be to set up a Research Council for Complementary Medicine. The Roundstreet Project was just the sort of thing they were interested in and there was every prospect that funds would be available to meet the cost of Dr Nobel-Mathew's participation.

Experience has taught me that if one leaves a problem to the Guv'nor he will sort it out in the end, and that confidence was now being justified. It also encourages me to believe that another dream of mine will one day be realized, the idea for a Healing Home.

So many people need the regular and repeated healing which I know to be necessary in many cases, yet are prevented by distance or other circumstances from coming regularly. For others the journey is not possible at all and they never receive healing. The Healing Home would solve this. People could come and stay there and receive regular healing. It would be in a house adjacent to my home, and I have my eye on a suitable property. My sister Pamela would come from the nursing home at Crawley, where she is Matron, to be Matron of the Healing Home. A friend of mine has already offered to run the business side. Donations would be channelled through a registered charity which could take the maximum advantage of the available tax concessions.

I have no idea where the funds for this are going to come from, but one thing I do know — take one step towards the Guv'nor and he will take a hundred towards you.*

The pattern of Healing

Now, after eight years as a healer, my days have settled into a pattern. During that time I have seen about two thousand patients. That may seem few compared with the hundreds of thousands of a Harry Edwards, a Don Greenbank or a Tom Pilgrim. Each healer has his own style and mine involves giving each patient a lot of time and when necessary seeing them over a long period.

That is one reason why I do not belong to any of the associations of spiritual or faith healers. I avoid the word 'spiritual' because it is used by those who link their healing with some particular religion, and I do not. Nor is 'faith' applicable, because healing may be effective even for those who have no faith. Even the word 'nature' has misleading associations of the 'back to nature' kind. I call myself simply — a healer.

During those five years I have changed greatly. I have become very different from the chap who once managed three garages. I have come to understand better how healing works and how I can best fulfil my part in the process. I would not say that I have developed a method or system; each patient is different and needs different handling. Nevertheless there is a pattern.

The most important thing when patients first come is to put them at their ease. I sit them down in the waiting-room and we have a long talk. I explain to them that the healing has very little to do with me, that I personally heal nobody. I am merely a channel through which the healing passes. The power of it is so enormous, I could not be responsible for the wonderful things that happen. Nor can I guarantee that anyone can be cured, because healing is never imposed. It is only offered, and in order

* This dream is now one big step closer. A Banker has come forward and agreed to arrange for the necessary funding. He is Mr Peter Wreyford, formerly Chairman and Managing Director of The Gresham Trust plc.

to be effective it must be accepted.

I usually go on to assure them that their beliefs will not affect the outcome in any way. If they want to discuss their religious and philosophical attitudes I am happy to do so, but this is not a prerequisite.

I often have a feeling of empathy with people at this initial meeting. I take a long look at them and as often as not I seem to know what frame of mind they are in and how I should approach them. Frequently they are in a state of stress, which is understandable if the whole panoply of orthodox medicine and the National Health Service had failed to cure them. Sometimes I need to be serious, but at other times they may be put at their ease by a joke. During this preliminary talk I often begin to know what it is they need. In a sense the healing has started already.

The healing-room is beyond the waiting-room. When the time comes we go in there and I ask them to sit on a fairly high leather-covered stool which is placed so that they are looking out through the window. It faces the garden and overlooks a pond. They can see the trees and sky beyond. During a healing session they may see a great deal more.

I tell them that all they have to do is relax physically and mentally. There is no need for clothing to be removed, other than heavy outer garments. Healing passes through light clothing and the sensation is just as if it was not there. Then I sit myself down in my old wooden chair, the one I was sitting in when I had the first intimation that I was a healer. I switch on the stereo to start the music, generally something tranquil which I have previously recorded. The music is for my benefit rather than the patient's. It helps me to relax too.

I exclude all things from outside; I try not to be distracted by noises or worries of any kind. I concentrate on the patient. Then I ask the Guv'nor for help for that person. I have learned that it is a waste of time to try and tell the Guv'nor what they need. I simply put the whole thing totally in his hands.

I would not say that I am in a state of unawareness. I am aware of the patient as a person and of their degree of tension. I am aware that they have a pain or disease in certain parts of their body. I am aware whether they are male or female.

I do not get up from my chair till I know that the healing is there. Sometimes I can feel it beginning and yet I wait for it to get stronger before I move. In such cases the patient often experiences healing even before I stand up. Once again we are shown that the healing is not coming from the healer but only through him.

By the time I am standing behind the stool my hands have started to vibrate. For me this is no discomfort, though patients sometimes feel them as very hot or very cold. I always start with the shoulders and move to the head. After all, the head is the control room. It is the control room for effective design at work and through it healing can be channelled to correct the design where it has gone wrong.

I do not use any of the 'passes' that some exponents of healing teach. I do not manipulate limbs nor do I massage. In fact I hardly touch my patients, even though the touch of the healer does not hurt sore places.

There is great variation in what I do because patients' needs are varied. I move my hands to wherever it's necessary, but not always to the spot where the trouble is — or appears to be. Quite often they begin to receive healing at the trouble-spot before my hands are anywhere near it. Some have felt hands at the centres of pain — other hands, not mine. These unseen hands know exactly where to go. A patient who was coming to me regularly for treatment of her arm was suffering one day from an acute pain at the base of her spine. Accustomed to pain she did not mention this to me before healing started. Later she told me that while my hands were still above her head she felt her spine gripped by two strong fists at the place where it hurt. The pain went away.

My own experience differs from patient to patient. At times the healing seems so strong that I wonder how I can channel it; it is like a high-voltage electric current passing through a household lamp-flex. At other times I feel that the current has been weak and yet for the patient it has been strong. In the same way as I wait in my chair until the healing starts, so I go on till it stops. When the healing stops I turn the music off, wait for a little while and then go round to see what my patients' reactions are.

Usually they are in a bemused or an amazed or a very happy state. Often there is emotion, which can be deep. The sensations which they feel are very varied, often extraordinary. Some find themselves quite unable to express it in words. For others it is a private experience which they do not wish to share with anyone else, not even the healer.

Sometimes they do not realize they have been healed. I may have to tell them, for instance, to stand up and see if they can walk normally. Only then do they discover that they are better. Others know very well what has happened and one can see that a great weight has been lifted from them.

The healing that is given is tailored to meet the needs of the patient, the needs of the whole person at that time. Sometimes there is not the rapid improvement that we would like. An example of this was the woman deaf from birth who gained her hearing only gradually. She needed time to adjust and the healing power made allowances for this.

From time to time I am asked to give healing to people who for practical reasons are not able to come to Roundstreet — distant or absent healing. It is not so effective as direct healing but can be of great help. I do not arrange a kind of telepathic rendezvous with the person. If they have already been to see me I tell them to imagine themselves back on the stool in the healing room, as this makes it easier for them to concentrate their minds. Then all I do is sit down quietly and ask the Guv'nor to help them. There have been enough instances of effective absent healing for one to be sure that it can work, even to as distant a place as Australia. The healing power comes from far beyond me. It is all pervading and knows no barriers of distance or time.

Healing is wonderful in itself but it is a pointer to even bigger things. We must look not just at the fact of healing but seek to understand also the purpose of healing. Perhaps there is a clue in one of the questions posed by the Great Healer — a question to which no answer was forthcoming: 'Whether is it easier to say to the sick of the palsey, Thy sins be forgiven thee; or to say, Arise, take up thy bed and walk?'

Healing can be of great comfort to a person approaching death. It cannot avert death; we all must die. For one thing pain and suffering may be alleviated but more importantly the realization may dawn that death is not what it seems. Awareness of the creator spirit's loving concern, manifested through healing, is deeply reassuring. When a dying person comes to understand that the mortal body is no more than a vehicle for the immortal spirit he or she is able to look beyond death with confidence and hope.

How can I speak of healing when the patient is going to die and I know it? Because the true healing is for the spirit. And if the spirit is immortal how much more important it is that the spirit should be healed. The betterment of the physical body is simply a testimony to the enrichment of the spirit.

I was called once to the bedside of a man who was dying from cancer of the gullet. He was in great pain and distress of mind. Unable to swallow he could not eat, could not even drink anything. He was given healing. Afterwards he was free of pain and to the indignation of his doctor had his drugs and pain-killers thrown away. He was able to eat and drink with enjoyment. More important he had peace of mind. Death could not be averted, the time had come for him to die. But he died without pain and with a quiet mind.

Bereavement can be one of life's most cruel trials. It is often physically damaging. The mind's torment is echoed in physical disease. It may even be a cause of cancer. Here also healing can help. If it makes a mourner realize that the loved one's spirit cannot die and that they will be united again in the fullness of time then the destructive effects of grief may be lessened. There is loneliness, yes, but not the same sense of loss. If the most important part of us is not the body but the spirit then we cannot die. The purpose of our existence does not cease with death. Our spirit is not extinguished. And of this we have ample evidence.

I often tell the bereaved about my experiences after the death of my son Phillip. I wonder how many suicides that has prevented?

Some people are shocked because when talking about healing I refer to the Guv'nor. I chose this word for a reason. When one talks about God it conjures up the god of this or that particular religion or sect, with all the attributes that have been ascribed to him. God has other names in other religions and the same is true of them. We are here using words to talk about what cannot be described, only hinted at. There is a loving design behind human and cosmic life and that implies a loving designer — the creator, the source of all things, the great spirit. I do not find it easy to use these phrases in ordinary conversation. I have to use the word which for me does the job, expresses what I mean.

No one religion can have a monopoly of the truth. All religions are, or should be, striving towards spiritual truth and the way to a better life. My upbringing was Christian but I cannot accept some of the fundamental tenets of the Church's teaching. Spiritual understanding can be expressed only imperfectly in words. I think that man-made Church dogma has done much to obscure what the great healer Jesus Christ meant to convey by His life and sayings.

A man must base his belief on his own experience, then he *knows* rather than believes, though he can never know it all. If he thinks he does he is making the greatest mistake of all. I have my convictions but I am still searching for truth. I have no religion in the accepted sense of the word. Religion formulates rules and suggests a system of sanctions and rewards, whereas I believe that God has infinite kindliness and understanding of our weakness. This does not mean that I think all things are permissible, but I find it hard to give credence to the idea that we have to ask God for forgiveness. I do not see God as someone who needs to forgive, rather as one who has endless patience with our stupidities.

Nor do I believe that we have four score years of life on earth and are judged by our performance during the allotted span, reaping the rewards or paying the penalty during an ensuing eternity. Life on earth is not some sort of test with an assessment of our performance after we die. We are here to learn and that is what this life is all about. There is a law of cause and effect, expressed in the words: 'Ask, and it shall be given you; seek, and ye shall find; knock and it shall be opened unto you . . .'

Man is not a body with a spirit, he is a spirit with a body. The non-material spirit is more important than the material body. It matters more because it is not bounded by time, it is eternal. There is more to our existence than life in the physical world. If this life is stressful it is for a reason; we are here to learn.

After all, what is the body? A solid? There is no such thing as a solid. Scientists researching the nature of matter have penetrated the atom and are probing the sub-atomic universe. They have found that within the atom are regions of space where infinitesimal particles move at unimaginable speeds. It is a universe where known physical laws no longer make sense. As their instruments for monitoring the sub-atomic universe become more powerful they have begun to detect at the very core of matter what can only be described as a vibration akin to the vibrations associated with human thought.

At the end of the road will the abstract and the material turn out to be one and the same? Are not all artefacts examples of thought in action? A craftsman-built chair existed first in a man's mind. I can see the universe as a thought in the mind of God — before the Creation. 'In the beginning was the word'. I realize that Genesis is accepted as an allegory or a vision but knowing the power of the Creator I believe that it *could* have been done in six days.

What *is* Healing?

So we come to the crux of this whole book. What *is* healing?

I will try to describe something which may make it easier for those with a practical turn of mind to understand. When a piano tuner strikes his A fork it vibrates at 440 cycles per second. If the piano's A string above middle C is in tune, that is to say at the right combination of length and tension, it too will start resonating or vibrating in response to the sound waves emitted by the fork. If there is another piano in the room and somebody's foot is on the sustaining pedal its A string will also start to vibrate. The important thing about this process is that *energy is transferred.* When two elements are in vibrational harmony energy can pass from one to the other even if the frequencies are different. For instance, a loud A will cause audible vibrations on the A string in the next octave, which vibrates at 880 cycles per second or twice as fast.

Not only vibrating piano strings respond to external cyclic stimuli. So do people. There is of course a greater range of sound than the human ear is capable of catching. In the practice of healing there is often much vibration running through the healer or in his hands, and this is felt by the patient. These vibrations have been described as corrective in that they restore harmony. The character of these vibrations differs to suit the different needs of each patient, and even with the same patient it may differ from one session to another.

The healing vibrations are not sound vibrations but are nonetheless energy or power being *intelligently* transmitted through the healer. The healer has little or no knowledge of what needs to be done to bring about the physical changes required for the particular ailment to be healed.

That is a practical analogy which throws some light on the

outward and physical signs of what is an inward and spiritual happening. An effective healer must develop a true understanding of love, and he must listen to the spiritual teaching available, to the instructions from within. This state has to be achieved by first divesting oneself of preconceived ideas and prejudices and remembering simply that God is love and that we are all part of Him and of one another. I am given help in many different ways. The Guv'nor has many messengers. In some religions they are called 'angels', which means the same thing. That is why at weekends I sometimes seek guidance in my work by sitting quietly with a group of chosen friends waiting receptively for any messages that may come. A healer needs to know that he has this support.

One cannot be a healer without becoming intimately aware of the loving designer who created us and who cares so deeply about us. His love is the most powerful force there is and healing is love itself in action. It is effective design at work.

As Edgar Cayce, the American healer, said: 'The spirit is the life, the mind is the builder and the body is the result.' Where there is harmony between spirit, mind and body you have real health. Disease occurs when that harmony is broken.

Broken it often is by the process of living. You have only to look at the ravages of time on the faces of some people to have proof that living is stressful. Yet the greater the stress the greater the chance to learn. Illness, or bereavement, or the approach of death provide an opportunity for learning in greater depth. Healing is indeed wonderful in itself but it is a pointer to even bigger things. We must look not just at the fact of healing but seek to understand also the purpose of healing.

What is healing? What is its purpose? To those two questions there is one answer: healing is evidence of the great spirit's love.

The healing power passes from the Great Spirit
through the healer's spirit to the spirit of the patient.
Within the patient it takes the route SPIRIT-MIND-BODY.
Thus the healing passes from spirit through spirit to spirit
and is reflected in mind and body.

Comprehending this evidence of the Great Spirit's love is more important than a physical cure. For many the experience of healing is a turning-point in their lives. It points them in a new direction. That direct contact with the power and the glory may for some be cataclysmic. The realization of what healing is and what lies beyond it can bring about a complete change in a person's attitude to life.

Roundstreet House
Wisborough Green
Sussex

They Came to be Healed

by James McConnell

The first part of this book gave an account of healing from the point of view of the healer himself. The second part is written from a detached and independent standpoint. It offers a sample of the experiences of some twenty people who came to Phil Edwardes for healing. If there was enough space hundreds more could have been described and extraordinary new healings are being reported every week.

The following accounts are not intended to provide scientific evidence. Medical research would require much more detailed monitoring of each case throughout all its stages. Such a study would require a great deal of time and money, and the researcher would need to have access to medical records which are not available to the layman. With the establishment of the Research Council for Complementary Medicine such investigations may become possible. In the meantime these stories do amount to an interesting, perhaps even convincing body of evidence. The writer heard them from patients' own lips and has recorded the facts simply as they were told to him. To ensure accuracy the versions as printed have each been submitted to the person in question for checking and verification. Many are ongoing cases which will continue to develop in further interesting ways after this book has gone to press.

Any reader who finds it hard to believe Phil Edwardes' own account of successful healings will here find corroborative evidence. Although some impressions were shared by all or nearly all the patients, these stories are as varied as the people who told them. Each has its own particular interest and flavour, with sometimes a startling and unique experience.

* *DISEASE:* (from Latin *dis*, not and French *aise*, ease): any deviation from health; disorder in any part of the mind or body.

JUNE GUNN

Disease: Accident injuries, vertebrae compounded, discs dislodged, pain.

'My God, I don't believe it!'

The first part of June Gunn's story was told at the beginning of the book. It goes on to a happy ending.

When she returned home after the first visit to Phil Edwardes she had several blissful days free of pain. Then it struck again. Max immediately phoned Phil and arranged to take her back to Roundstreet.

Once again the healing was effective and this time the betterment lasted longer.

She went on going to see him regularly for the next eight months. During that period she had no other medical treatment. But the specialist at Worthing had arranged for her to go back to him for monthly check-ups. By the end of June her condition was so improved that he told her she need not come back till September.

Meanwhile progress under Phil was uneven. Pain in varying degrees came and went. One night she had a bad fright. She was woken up by an intense pain at the top of her back. It was a new pain she had not felt before. She thought, 'I'm paralysed again.' She made herself get up, called Max. Max came to rub her back with soothing lotion, as he often did.

He said, 'My God, I don't believe it!'

He had not told June that all this time one vertebra had been protruding from the upper part of her spine. Now it had slipped back into place of its own accord. This had caused the sharp pain, which soon subsided.

At about this time Phil suggested that she should try and give up the Valium. With her usual dogged determination she complied. She suffered withdrawal symptoms but won independence from the drug.

Healing had been asked for her back. She knew that her left knee was hopeless. After all it had been locked in its bent position for one third of a century. During those months of healing the left knee gradually loosened. It became free and flexible, though the cap remained mushy. Now she can demonstrate a full knees bend and stretch the leg out straight.

She went back to Worthing in September for the next six-monthly check-up. Her specialist pronounced her cured. There was no need, he said, for her to come back any more.

She did not tell him that she owed her cure to a healer.

Of her experience of healing she says, 'To begin with I did not feel much but gradually things got better. As time went on I began to feel the healing even before Phil stood up. The healing always seemed to go right to the spot where it was most needed. Phil would put his hand on my spine and as he got to the damaged place my body would light up inside. The healing went right to the root of the problem.'

Even when she was pronounced cured she went on going to Phil. She knew that her nerves had taken a terrible punishing and during this later phase it was to her nerves that the healing was directed. Many people do not stay the course. They become better but not totally cured. June was sure that she had to receive healing regularly over a long period and continue with it even after she seemed 'better'.

Now, more than a year after the last healing session, she is leading a normal life. She has a part-time job as a clerk. She drives a car. She does the housework. She walks the dogs. The only thing she denies herself is riding; that might be pushing her luck too far.

And she has learned to control her own mind and to control pain. If she suffers pain she thinks about the part that is hurting. Her own hand becomes warm. She puts it on the part and the pain goes away.

Here is a person who had come to the end of the road where

orthodox medicine was concerned. She was crippled and in constant pain but with the best will in the world there was nothing more the doctors could do for her. No blame on them. They were faced with an apparently incurable condition.

Thanks to the enlightenment and flexible attitude of her GP she went to a healer and was completely cured. This must surely be of the greatest interest to all whose vocation is to care for the sick.

SIMON WEIR

Disease: Tumours on neck; suspected cancer.

'Give or take I'd say it was a miracle.'

Simon is the son of a cruise director who spends seven months of every winter on a luxury liner in the Caribbean. At the age of sixteen he is already an inch and a half over six foot. His brother is two years older and tops him by two inches. They live in West Chiltington, Sussex.

Simon has the angled, rangy movements of one who has grown rapidly. He talks enthusiastically, illustrating his point with gestures of his expressive hands.

He goes to Steyning Grammar School where he is preparing to take six O-level subjects. His favourite sports are water-skiing and football, and he represents the school for the latter. His ambition is to become an actor and he very much wants to be a student at the Royal Academy of Dramatic Art. He has already done a course in New Era Drama and has learnt stage techniques. Being realistic he plans to take a course in French cooking at Litlington near Newhaven. This will provide him with a diploma, so he will have a safety net should he need to earn his living other than by acting.

About Christmas time 1981 he became aware of a lump below and behind his right ear. It was not long before another one came up in the same area, by which time the first one was as hard as bone. This was very worrying as he had a friend who suffered from leukaemia. His doctor gave him a blood test and the first indications were that he had glandular fever. This diagnosis was altered after a second blood test, and he was sent for further examination and was finally passed on to the cancer specialist. The specialist did not like the look of the lumps, now as big as ping-pong balls. He said he would have to take them out and do a biopsy. An appointment was made for the operation to be done.

By this time Easter had come and gone. Back at school Simon's friends kept making very frank comments on the unsightly lumps on his neck. Needless to say his mother was extremely worried and Simon admits that he himself was getting 'really panicky'.

It was a few months before this that the TV programme *The Medicine Men* had been shown. His mother had watched the film which dealt with healing and saw Phil Edwardes in action. Next day she'd gone out and bought the book based on the series. Now, using the information given there, she discovered Phil Edwardes's telephone number and rang him up. An appointment was made for a day one week before the operation was due.

Simon was quite happy to go along with the idea of healing. 'Well, great!' he thought. 'This might work.'

His mother drove him to Roundstreet House. He felt immediately comfortable, it was so unlike hospital. When he met Mr Edwardes there was immediate friendship. The three of them sat down and had a really long talk, about an hour. Only during the last fifteen minutes did they get onto the subject of the lumps. Then Simon went into the healing-room while his mother waited in the room outside. Sitting on the stool he was a little nervous. This was the end of a twelve-week period during which the lumps had been getting worse and worse.

When Mr Edwardes put his hand over his head he felt 'as if there was a form of radiation heat in vibration waves'. An extraordinary sensation went down the whole of his right side from his ear to his toe and down his left arm. He felt his eyes flickering and drooping and was overcome by an incredible feeling of relaxation. His mind had gone blank but he was aware of the heat coming from Mr Edwardes's hands. The strange thing was that the heat felt just as strong on the parts which were covered by clothes as it did on his bare skin.

Waiting in the room outside his Mum also felt the warmth.

When Simon and Phil came out of the healing room they were both, she said, 'on a complete high', though Phil looked drained.

That night after returning home Simon still felt the warmth and was still on a complete high.

During the following six days the hardness gradually went out of the lumps and they became more like fat. When he went to see Mr Edwardes again it was just one day before the operation.

This time there was again the flickering of his eyes and the feeling of warmth. But now heat was coming from his neck as well as into it. 'There was penetration all the way through; it was as if the lumps in my neck were of butter and the heat was melting it.'

The next morning they had gone down like a pricked balloon. During that day they gradually went away and became just like a fatty cyst.

Simon's father had come back from the Caribbean and his parents agreed that there was no point now in going ahead with the operation. They rang the hospital and invented a white lie to cancel it.

The lumps disappeared completely in about fourteen days and he never had any further treatment for them.

Simon's comment: 'Give or take, I'd say it was a miracle.'

In fact the experience has had a profound effect on his character. He recognizes that something has happened to change his whole attitude to life.

GEORGE AND MABEL ALLEN

Diseases: Rheumatoid arthritis;
phlyctenular conjunctivitis, sciatica.

'Nothing else gives me the same relief and help as healing. And I mean help in a special sense.'

Professor Allen and his wife live in a neat little terraced house on the east side of a steeply sloping street in Lewes. There are two deepish steps up to the front door. Fixed to the wall on the left is a handrail.

Professor Allen is a tall man, well over six feet, still erect at the age of seventy-four. He has a clean-shaven face that tapers to the chin, very keen but sympathetic grey-blue eyes. His voice is soft but clear, his brain unimpaired. He speaks in a measured, precise way. A meeting with him is a thoughtfully planned affair which follows a predetermined timetable. The planning allows fifteen minutes at the end of the discussion for a drink, expertly mixed by Mrs Allen.

Mrs Allen wears a trouser suit. Her face is smiling and pleasant. Her hands are knobbly and twisted by rheumatoid arthritis. She explains that her elbows, cervical region, shoulders and knees, if you could see them, are just as bad. She walks with a rocking, stiff-legged motion. She does not complain, although she is never completely free from pain.

George Allen read both classics and English during his five years at Trinity College, Oxford. As an undergraduate he had as his tutor H. H. Price, the author of a book on perception. The book and its author had a profound influence on him. After leaving Oxford in 1932 he went to Germany as *lektor* at Hamburg University. This was the year Hitler came to power and as George hated Nazism he left Germany in 1934. During this year he had acquired fluent German. In 1937 he took up the work which was to be a major occupation of his life; he entered His Majesty's Inspectorate of Schools. In 1938 he married Mabel, a colleague whose subject was Physical Education. They have three sons currently living in New York, Blackheath and Vienna. The 1939-45 war found him in the Ministry of Health. When it ended he went back to the Inspectorate and in 1951 was sent to the Control Commission in Germany where he followed in the footsteps of Robert Birley as Educational Adviser to the UK High Commissioner. He spent three years in this work of regenerating education in a Germany which had been devastated morally and physically.

Back in England with the Inspectorate he became Staff Inspector for English and in 1956 was part of the team of H.M. Inspectors who visited Eton College, where Robert Birley was now Headmaster.

In 1966 he retired from the Inspectorate and was appointed Professor of Education at the recently-opened University of

Sussex. He filled this position, a rewarding one, for eight years before finally retiring in 1974. Since then he has kept his mind sharp by writing poetry. That this is effective is shown by his obviously alert and retentive mind, characteristic of a classical scholar.

Mabel and he came to live in Lewes in 1960. There she became a Borough Councillor for three years and a Brighton magistrate for much longer. She was also a member of the Committee on Sport set up by the Central Council for Physical Recreation.

It was in 1976 that Mabel contracted rheumatoid arthritis. The first intimation of the disease was when she woke up one morning to find her hands burning hot. She visited a London consultant who was also attached to a well-known teaching hospital. The treatment prescribed involved the use of a wide range of drugs, and the progress of the chemotherapy was to make these progressively stronger. Having earlier had a gastric ulcer, she could not tolerate aspirins. The treatment also included a cortisone injection given simultaneously in both arms, and the intense pain which this caused came without warning.

Her specialist said that he would like to have her in hospital for a week of observation. Once in hospital she manifested bizarre symptoms and had to be treated for these as opposed to the arthritis, with a change of consultants. Her mind began to wander and it was evident that the hospital was having to dry her out from the effects of the drugs which had been prescribed.

The result of this experience was to decide both of them never again to resort to drugs of any kind for the arthritis; one exception however was Indocid as some relief from acute pain.

Mabel now tried first massage then acupuncture. This brought temporary relief but the pain began to return each time after about half an hour.

At this point George happened to meet Mrs Molly Morgan, whose experience is related in another part of this book. She suggested that Mabel should go and see Phil Edwardes. Though Molly told how she had been healed of her migraines as well as her back and arm problems Mabel remained sceptical, only agreeing to visit the healer in order to please George. Her first visit was on 11 May 1980. From then on for a long period she went every week, but during the winter of 1981/2 she reduced this to once a fortnight. The only major break during this period was the couple's annual visit to Bad Gestein in the Austrian Alps.

Here one gets spa treatment with baths in hot spring water, which is mildly radioactive and good for rheumatic diseases.

Although healing has not noticeably improved her condition it has kept the disease stable. The great benefit that she gets is relief from pain. After a healing session this lasts for three days or so, a vast improvement on acupuncture and certainly preferable to drugs. These merely dulled her mind whereas healing has the opposite effect. Indeed for Mabel Allen the important thing about the healing is the sense of well-being she receives: 'It enables me to live with my infirmity. Nothing else gives me the same relief and help as healing. And I mean help in a special sense.'

Certainly old friends and members of the family who live abroad and see her intermittently agree that she looks far better now than three years ago, whereas normal clinical prognosis would expect the disease to get worse. Anyone meeting her for the first time sees her as a cheerful, outgoing and positive person.

Even so she has had no other treatment since she first went to Phil. After her 1981 visit to Bad Gastein she decided that she was well enough to go it alone and that she need not be dependent on regular visits to the healer. All too quickly the pain returned most cruelly. A visit to Roundstreet House was rapidly arranged and gave relief. She now had proof that the healing was doing much to keep the disease at bay.

George Allen would consider his experiences rather small beer as compared to his wife's. None the less they interested him profoundly and he has a sharp recollection of what happened.

In 1981 he began to suffer from an inflammation of the eyes known as phlyctenular conjunctivitis, a most uncomfortable complaint. Since the antibiotic ointment prescribed by his GP did not help it was arranged that he should see an eye specialist in Brighton. Weeks passed and still no appointment materialized. Meanwhile he was taking Mabel every week to see Phil Edwardes, who suggested on one of these visits — it was 12 March 1981 — 'Why don't you let me have a try, George, and see if there is any healing for you?'

So this time Mabel waited in the room next door while George sat on the high stool facing the window.

During the first treatment he did not experience anything remarkable. He had a sense of well-being and was surprised at the heat which he felt emanating from Phil's hands.

The second session eight days later was more interesting. He had the illusion that the healer's hands were making his hair curl, yet George is bald on the top of his head. The sensation became three-dimensional. Phil's hands seemed to 'fuse with the top of my scalp, as if they were actually digging into it'. He felt a burning heat in the healing hands and commented on this. Phil invited him to feel his hands, which were cool, of a perfectly normal temperature. And they had not at any point been in contact with George's scalp.

On the journey home, whenever George thought about it again he could feel the same heat at the back of his head, and this sensation continued for the rest of that day.

By the next visit on 27 April the eye was considerably better. The awareness of healing and the sense of well-being were strong. There was something else. He would not go so far as to say that his mind or spirit had at any time moved out of his body. He used a Greek phrase to describe the experience. Translated this means, 'My psyche is all of a flutter.' On this and several subsequent occasions he had, he said with a smile, 'gone extremely light at my moorings'. He felt that he was spontaneously rising up in his chair — 'A mental state but no less real for that.'

On 2 May there was a strong vibration which originated in Phil's hands and extended to George's shoulders. The eye had improved further. During the following week his turn for an appointment with the eye man in Brighton came up. The specialist gave George's eye the customary inspection. After some thought he pronounced his verdict: 'Phlyctenular conjunctivitis is not always easy to deal with, and you had it all right. Now it's just about gone and your eyes are now in perfectly good shape.'

He charged his usual fee and the Professor went on his way. He had no other treatment from orthodox medical agencies. After two more visits to Phil his eye was completely cured. There has been no relapse.

A year later to the day he was back at Roundstreet House. He had strained his back shifting sacks of leaf mould in the garden. Now instead of going to a doctor his reaction was to telephone Phil. It seemed to be a sciatic problem, something to do with the sacroiliac joint. As usual, Phil did not attempt to make a medical diagnosis, simply to locate the seat of the trouble and direct healing towards it. He himself did not feel that the healing had been very strong that day but his patient was aware of an immediate improvement — 'I felt a stone lighter, as if a great weight had been lifted from me.'

A week later Phil sensed an increase in the healing and his patient commented that he felt the inflammation being taken out of his back.

In March his right foot began to give trouble. There was pain in his ankle and in the arch of his foot behind the toes. He had difficulty in walking. Back to Phil Edwardes, whose notes record that the patient felt great heat in the ankle, as well as in the head and shoulders. Even when the healing session had ended this heat persisted and it returned on the two following visits. There was again that lessening of earthly awareness, and along with the healing, the familiar feeling of being uplifted, of being far away and noting himself as a small figure sitting on the stool in the healing room.

At the end of May Professor Allen went off to Austria for a month's walking in the mountains.

ELIZABETH ADSHEAD

Disease: Loss of arm movement.

'. . . as though the Amazon had burst its banks and the flood waters were pouring down over me . . .'

When Liz was nineteen she was in a car accident. She was sitting in the back seat and got badly smashed up. She does not remember anything about it, and it is understandable if she does not want to. The accident changed the course of her life.

Over the years — more than two score of them — she had undergone all sorts of treatment to put her right. She was, as she puts it, 'in the healing orbit'. None of the cures, conventional or unconventional, could alter the fact that her body from below the arms was paralysed and devoid of feeling. A resolute character and an acute mind has enabled her to create a meaningful life for herself, but everything she does depends on the use of her arms.

She has a very alive face, slightly quizzical, with large expressive eyes and a mouth that is very ready to smile. Her eyes take on a far-away look when she begins to talk about Phil Edwardes and healing.

She cannot walk, so her waking hours are spent in a sitting posture. She sleeps lying face downwards. She uses a wheelchair to get about the house. She can go out to the garage in her wheelchair, but needs help to transfer herself to the car. The car is fitted with special controls, so once at the wheel she is free and independent. This greatly extends her range and enriches her life.

She lives with her mother and a helper in a bungalow just off the main road in Fittleworth. In her own room she sits, legs in blue trousers stretched out on the bed, facing a broad window overlooking the road. She has a cushion on her lap and another at the bottom of the bed for her poodle to lie on. Suspended from the ceiling so that it dangles in front of her head is a triangle. She can grasp this and support her weight when she wants to shift her position. To get out of bed she needs help.

Bookcases line the walls, though she says she does not have much time to read. Within easy reach are the controls of her radio and cassette recorder. Also close at hand are the telephone and the Citizen Band radio which the local CB club presented to her. She has, of course, her own code-name on CB and can chat to other 'breakers'. Lying flat on her face at night she can operate these two lines of communication to the outside world with her left hand.

There is also a dangling cord. This is important. It operates the door so that she can let her four dogs in and out. Hanging on the walls or from the bookshelves are many pictures of dogs.

She has a number of activities. She makes many recordings of music. She helps at the local infant school by listening to five-year-olds reading aloud. She provides a local delivery service; her mobility in the car enables her to do this. But the mere business of living occupies a lot of time. Getting up in the morning and going to bed at night, for instance, takes hours.

That was the pattern of her life up till June 1982. She had suffered for it and made it into a meaningful existence. But all this was now threatened. A deterioration in her condition had become apparent. She was beginning to lose movement in her left arm. She could no longer operate the telephone and CB controls from her face-down position in bed. Sitting up, she could not operate, for instance, the device for letting the dogs in and out. She was beginning to need much more help getting in and out of bed. Worst of all she was not able to drive herself in the car. Her horizons were being drastically narrowed.

On 14 June she drove to the hospital to have an X-ray. The verdict given was that 'she was fine'; there were no nerves trapped, nothing showing up on the X-ray. She went to see her osteopath. He could do nothing for her.

'Till this,' she said, 'I was going pretty well on two wings. Now all feeling had gone from my left arm. I could not even get my hand off the deck.'

Sunday, 20 June, was her most desperate day. Her condition was getting daily worse. The telephone was her lifeline and she could not use it. She could not lift the food to her mouth, the steak she was trying to eat went in her lap. She was needing more attention than she could ask her mother to give. She tried to face the fact that she could not stay in her home, and would have to go to some kind of institution.

Friends had told her about the healing given by Phil Edwardes. Though she had tried so many things already she was interested enough to feel like giving it a chance. She rang Phil up and made an appointment.

On 22 June 1982 she was taken to Roundstreet House by her great friend Sally Inman. Sally is a State Registered Nurse. They arrived at Phil's about four-thirty. There had been rain in the morning. Sally got her into the wheelchair and pushed her into the waiting-room. She felt a little bit scared. Phil talked to her for a while. He said she did not need to have any belief or faith. All she had to do was relax.

He wheeled her into the healing-room and parked her, still in the chair, facing the window. She could see the pond beyond the garden. Swifts were screaming around and swooping low. Phil put the music on and after a while he stood up behind her. She was aware of his hands moving close to her head and shoulders. They were fluttering rather like butterflies.

She felt goodness dropping down on her in a flood . . . It was as if the Amazon had burst its banks and the flood waters were pouring down over her in a cataract of goodness through her whole body . . . It was like being in a tropical rain forest . . . She did not actually cry but tears simply poured from her eyes and flowed down her cheeks. The music was playing but — it wasn't the music . . .

When Liz came out she was changed. She had been so low both physically and mentally when she went in; she came out elated, one could almost say radiant. The colour of everything seemed unnaturally bright and vivid. Most important of all she had arm movement. Phil, by contrast, looked grey and drained, though he maintained he felt no fatigue.

Sally thought: 'Oh, if only I could persuade my father to come and see this man.' Her father is a sufferer from rheumatoid arthritis. Since then she has suggested to several people whose illnesses are not yielding to treatment that they should go to a healer.

When Liz got home her mother commented: 'Something's happened to Liz.'

That night she tested her left arm. She found she was able not only to reach the telephone but to hold her hand four inches above it.

On her second visit she experienced so many things that it was hard to describe. Again she felt the goodness pouring over her. However, owing to the high back of the chair, Phil was only able to reach her shoulders and the very top of her spine. Yet the base of her spine was eased.

All that she had asked for was arm movement, yet healing was being given to the whole area of her spine.

On her third visit, when Phil's hands were fluttering at the back of her neck but not actually touching her, she felt 'as if a laser beam was going through the back of my neck reaching my spine.'

By 13 July she was able to drive herself to Roundstreet. It was noticeable that there was less strain on her face. She was able to move her back away from the chair-back so that Phil could work a hand's span down from her neck. And at home she was able to do more to help people move her.

The visits for healing had now become a regular weekly feature of her life and continued thus right through till the summer and autumn. The atmosphere of Roundstreet House was amazingly comforting; she was always aware of a loving presence that was more than the presence of Phil. As soon as the music started, even before he approached her, she could feel a tingling in her body.

On a recent visit she had felt impelled to sit up straight in the wheelchair. Then she felt the healing going to the lower part of her back. That is an area where she had no true sensation except of discomfort and of course Phil's hands could not reach it. But she felt as if a warm pad was being pressed against that part.

When all this sort of thing was happening, she felt *five* pairs of hands working over her. (Phil's hands were still at the back of her head.) She felt as if these five pairs of hands were holding her rib cage and massaging and working over the muscles of her tummy. These were the muscles which had atrophied because of the posture she had been committed to for so long. It was a strong, almost violent sensation. That evening sitting on her bed she still felt that she had been worked over in a strong and positive way. She said to herself: 'Oh, that feels good!'

About a month later, when waiting to see Phil, she felt pain low down in her back. She did not tell Phil about it; she wanted him to concentrate on her arm. When healing started, with Phil's hands as usual at the back of her head, she felt two fists holding the hurting part together.

'The pain stopped. It just stopped hurting.'

She had no other treatment during the period from June till October. Yet she had been able to resume all her old activities and go on living in her own home. Thanks to healing. The simple statement: 'I know what I couldn't do before and what I can do now,' says it all.

MOLLY MORGAN

Disease: Migraines, damaged spine, crushed nerve in arm.

'You don't *garden,* do you?'

Molly Morgan is rising sixty, an intelligent, cultivated and alert woman. She was a WREN in World War II. Her husband was in the Foreign Service and she spent twenty years with him in the Far East. The demands of the job were too great and their marriage failed. They are now divorced, and he has another wife and family. Molly has three daughters and five grandchildren.

She has always been the kind of person who prefers to be alone rather than amidst the babble of conversation. She loves walking by herself, especially in mountainous country. She has walked all through Nepal and extensively in Israel, India and Western Tibet.

A few years ago, under the guidance of her friend and godmother, a GP, she became a Roman Catholic.

She now lives at Denne Park, just north of Horsham. It is a former stately home, converted into sixteen flats. The approach is up a half-mile straight avenue flanked by swards and a double row of lime trees.

Her present job is as a children's escort with British Caledonian Airways. She escorts parties of up to eighty children to destinations abroad. She has to give the job up in January as she has reached the age limit.

Since the age of fourteen she has suffered from migraines. Only those who have experienced this affliction know what it means — not just headaches but a sickening agony that shoots through the whole brain. Attacks could last up to eighteen hours. During that time she'd be sick every quarter of an hour. Being sick was no relief but an increase of torment. If an attack hit her on a trip abroad she would have to abandon the trip and lie up till the pain passed. But she had learned to live with migraines.

Fifteen years ago she developed severe back trouble. Her spine was crumbling. She experienced the indescribable degree of pain which is associated with this condition. She had an operation called a laminectomy (a sort of fusing of the spine). Four vertebrae were taken out.

For the next five months she was bedridden. The surgeon had to re-operate as she had grown a network of adhesions in her back.

After coming to live at Denne Park she attended the lecture on healing given by Phil Edwardes in Horsham Town Hall. A woman sitting behind her stood up at the end and told how she had been cured of migraines by a healer. Afterwards Molly stayed to talk to Phil. As a devout Catholic she needed reassurance on one point. Did he think that the healing gift came from himself or did he believe it was God-given? Phil told her, smiling: 'I do nothing. If there is any healing it's done by the Guv'nor. Why don't you come along and we'll see what we can do?'

Satisfied by this answer, she went to see him the following Monday.

On that first visit she did not feel anything particular inside herself. She was aware that his hands on her head were going hot and then cold.

The following week she felt a migraine starting. She rang up Phil, told him: 'I can get to you but I may not be able to get home.'

He said: 'Come at once.'

On the way to Roundstreet in the car the migraine was very bad. She was continuously being sick. When she arrived she did not care whether she lived or died. Somehow she got into the healing-room. Phil sat her on the stool. He put his hands on her head. After ten minutes the headache was gone and she had stopped feeling sick. She was no longer the pain-demented creature who had stumbled into the healing-room but a normal person.

She went to see him once more. Since then she has had three years free of migraines.

A year after the migraines were cured she had a fall and broke her arm in two places. The nerve was crushed. Her doctors took measurements and told her that it would take twenty-two months for the nerve to grow. The speed of growth of nerves damaged in this way is a statistic known to medical science.

Molly was contemplating twenty-two months of severe pain.

She went to see Phil. She walked into the healing-room literally crying with pain. She came out smiling. She has had no pain since.

She went to see her doctors to tell them that her arm was cured. They were sceptical and made dismissive remarks about newfangled medicine.

One doctor who was intensely interested was her friend Dr Noble-Mathews. Subsequently she advised a number of her own patients to see Phil Edwardes and became closely associated with him.

Molly said: 'If I get ill again I won't go to the doctor, I'll go to Phil. But actually,' as an afterthought, 'I don't get ill.'

She had not even mentioned to Phil that she had a back problem. But it was cured at the same time. There is no evidence now of a crumbling spine. She does a full day's work in the big gardens of Denne Park. She can lift quite heavy objects. Friends say: 'You don't *garden,* do you? What about your back?'

In fact, she feels better than at any time in her whole life. She does not even suffer from jet lag after a long flight.

She has a sister called Sue, who is married to Mike and suffers from tension. They live in Australia. On their most recent visit to this country Molly persuaded Sue to come along and see Phil.

Mike said: 'It's nonsense. I don't believe in that sort of thing.'

'Just come,' Molly told him. 'There are no strings attached.'

Grudgingly, Mike went along too.

Sue went into the healing-room rather apprehensively. When she came out she was ecstatic and completely relaxed, as if she was on a trip after taking some psychedelic drug.

Mike was persuaded to go in, too. He had suffered from gout for fifteen years and there was no cure for that, certainly not from this odd-ball of a healer. As expected he felt nothing: 'There you are, I told you.'

But that evening, instead of the usual gyp from his big toe, he had no pain at all. That was two years ago and he has had no pain since.

Now he says: 'If ever I have gout again I'll take the next 'plane home and see Phil.'

Six months ago, out in Australia, Sue had leg pains. She rang Molly. Molly rang Phil.

'Tell her to imagine herself back on the stool in my healing-room.'

Molly did that and three days later Sue rang up to say that the pain had gone.

JOYCE FERGUS-ENGEL

Disease: Accidental injuries: fractured tibia and knee; complications, pain.

'Would you mind doing another lap of the surgery?'

Joyce lives with her husband Michael in Aldwick, a few miles west of Bognor Regis. She is in her early fifties, has fair hair, blue eyes and a warm, welcoming personality. Michael is tall and lean with strongly defined features and extraordinarily intense deep-set eyes.

They have a son aged thirty who went out to Israel and worked in a kibbutz till he met and married an Israeli girl. Paul was called up twice for military service in the recent troubles, but he disapproves of Begin's policies and is returning home.

The story of Michael's life is an unusual one and its strange quirks put Joyce on the road to the healing of Phil Edwardes.

Like Phil himself Michael was rejected by his natural parents and brought up by foster parents. During his early years he had a sense of not belonging. He was a man without any family background. At the age of sixteen he succeeded in locating his mother and father, and tried to get on terms with them. His mother seemed ready to acknowledge him but his father did not want to have anything to do with him. On leaving school he joined the Army for a few years, then switched to the Colonial Police in Malaya. On his return to England he worked for an oil company and it was he who was instrumental in getting Phil Edwardes the tenancy of the garage at Buck's Green in 1965.

Michael meanwhile had met and married Joyce, but he still had not found a job in which he could feel any satisfaction. A break came in 1972 when the refugees from Uganda began pouring into Britain. Michael's knowledge of the language was useful and he was appointed to run a refugee camp. In the nature of things that came to an end and he once more tried various jobs.

Before her accident Joyce had dabbled in journalism and done some scripts for the BBC but on the whole she was unmotivated for that type of work. Marriage and her family were her principal occupation.

It was about three years ago while she and Michael were living in a 200-year-old cottage in Buckingham that the accident happened. Joyce had sprained an ankle and was awkward in her movements. One Friday afternoon she went down to the basement, where the bathroom was, to take a bath. Michael, pottering about upstairs, began to be aware that she had been down there a long time. It was past six o'clock and darkness had fallen. He went down, found Joyce sitting on the edge of the bath, sobbing her heart out.

She had slipped when reaching for the tap and crashed athwart the bath, crumpling in a mess of broken bones. She was unable to walk but he managed to haul her to a bedroom in the basement and persuaded her to let him send for a doctor.

Her own doctor was away. His 'locum' eventually turned up. He looked at the terribly swollen leg and agreed that it was a bit puffy.

'Yes, well, you'd better get your wife into hospital,' he said to Michael, and departed.

Michael phoned for an ambulance, and was told that the ambulance had to be ordered by a doctor.

By the time he had gone through the approved procedures and the ambulance arrived it was 1 a.m. Joyce, screaming with pain, was taken to Stoke Mandeville Hospital. In basic terms she had a broken tibia and knee bone. They set the fracture and put her leg in plaster from thigh to ankle. She was taken back home early on Saturday morning.

She did not sleep during the whole of that weekend. The pain was too intense. The only way she could get relief was by lying on the floor holding her leg in the air by means of Michael's dressing-gown cord.

Michael did not sleep either.

On the Monday she was taken to Bletchley Hospital, where she was seen by a surgeon from Stoke Mandeville. The nerves had been trapped when the fractured tibia was set. She was taken back to Stoke Mandeville where she underwent an operation; a spinum pin was put through her knee.

She was kept in hospital, where she was given 'skeletal traction'. Despite its grim-sounding name this treatment was not efficacious. After a week the surgeon broke it to her that he would have to perform another operation.

It was at this point that an appalling realization came over her; she knew that all the optimism being shown by the medical staff was false and that they feared there was not much they could do.

'From now on I'm going to be some other kind of person.'

The operation was to open up her leg below the calf and try to poke the nerves back into life round the dropped foot-arch. This produced a lucky bonus, for a bad clot was found and removed.

She was in Stoke Mandeville for seven or eight weeks. During that time she met some wonderful people — doctors, nurses, porters and the voluntary drivers who were to ferry her to and from the hospital for treatment. She particularly remembers the moment when, waiting on a trolley outside the operating theatre, she looked up to see a kindly face above a clerical collar. It was a retired rural dean who made a practice of coming into the hospital to comfort people in great distress. He spoke words to her which were of great solace.

After leaving hospital she had physiotherapy every day for a year, then three times a week for a second year, and after that twice a week for a third year. Finally it came down to six-monthly visits to Stoke Mandeville for check-ups. The physiotherapy was not bringing any improvement and there was nothing more the doctors could do.

She had come to resign herself to a life not just as a cripple but a cripple in constant pain; someone who could not sleep much. She had been provided with a plastic boot which she wore at night. As it collected a lot of sweat and had to be emptied out Michael drilled holes in it so that it could drain. In the daytime she wore a man's medicinal boot but her foot was so swollen that the boot had to be cut so that she could get it on. She shuffled around with the aid of two sticks.

She could just about make it out to the car but life out of doors was impossible. She was totally flat. 'I had become the kind of person who does not dare to look forward. Tomorrow was far enough away.' What was hard to bear was the expression on the faces of people who had not seen her since the accident. She could read their expressions as they registered, 'Can this be Joyce, the Joyce we knew?'

But she never surrendered to pain-killers. She soldiered on, making those six-monthly visits to Stoke Mandeville for check-ups that revealed no improvement, only continuous deterioration.

Till the end of 1981.

In the autumn of that year Michael's attention had been called to a notice in the paper asking him to contact a firm of solicitors. He did so and discovered that his mother had died intestate, his father having died some years before. He was her sole heir and beneficiary and had thus inherited a fine detached house in Aldwick, a well-found residential suburb of Bognor Regis. It was a crucial happening for Michael because suddenly he was no longer a man without a background, he was a man who had inherited a house from his mother.

They came to live in it soon after the turn of the year. It made a considerable change from the cottage in Buckingham and Michael soon found a job which was just up his street. He became a private investigator.

He came home one day and said, 'I met Phil Edwardes today. He's now a full-time healer.'

Joyce was pleased to hear that Phil, after years of searching, had at last found his *métier*. She did not think of herself as ever going to a healer.

In 1979 a friend of hers called Julie had been healed at a session in a church but Joyce had declined. She did not feel that this was for her. 'There was nothing as hopeful as hope.'

Phil and Sue invited them as old friends to lunch at Roundstreet. After the meal she sensed that Phil wanted to try and help her.

He said, 'Would you like me to have a go, see if there's any healing for you?'

She thought, 'It's Phil, my friend,' and answered, 'Yes.'

An appointment was made for the following week and Michael drove her up.

Thanks to the diary she kept during all these years Joyce has been able to provide a personal account of what happened.

> *16 April 1982* First treatment session with PE. Very strange sensation of warmth. An immediate feeling of lost strength, like a memory sharply renewed, and an ease in the totally stiff ankle. Later very sleepy, and on advice from PE let the sleepiness take over and went to bed.
>
> The next day awoke with a completely peaceful feeling, as if the tonic effect of really deep sleep, without a background of pain, had been a mere memory. Suddenly, I realized that this indeed was so. I had forgotten what it was like to sleep soundly and free from pain.

During that first week made very happy 'discoveries'. Each one a tiny, taken-for-granted thing, but a rich experience for one who did not know that she had 'lost' so many small freedoms: that I had not touched my sticks or the medicinal boot since coming home last Friday evening; that I wanted to pop across the road to take a book to a friend, and did so.

The second visit to PE a week later resulted in a dramatic change in my knee. The strange 'cheesey' shape and oedema just were not there. The injured knee now matched the other one. I could swing-a-leg with enjoyment for myself, even if causing alarm or amusement for others. Such joy in suppleness.

The third visit resulted in renewed feeling of the foot being in contact with the ground. Very tender and sometimes painful, but *feeling*. Sudden spasms of movement in the toes. I walked on the stony beach with pleasure in place of fear. My foot began to look more like a foot and less like a flipper.

After my fourth visit to PE, the by now usual feeling of sleepiness made me lie down on the sofa when we got home. As I did so, there was a vicious pain inside my foot. I was breathless with the intensity of the pain. PE had prepared me for the possibility of this and also I had read many case histories. I allowed the pain to do its work and hobbled upstairs to bed. Again, that marvellous sleeping and waking so refreshed. The stiff gungeyness of the foot much reduced and giving lateral flexibility in the ankle. No pain when walking.

During the weeks that followed, every single improvement was maintained and developed. A gentle and perfect logic apparent, in that the adaptations to 'normal' living are as difficult to adjust to as the original crippling of our bodies, with the great and wonderful difference that it is a happy experience.

Weeks of the ability to walk further and feel less tired followed, always with noticeable improvement in shape, size, and circulation. A blissful day when, for the first time in three years, I went into a shoe shop and picked a pair of high-heeled sandals off the rack and put them on and walked out in them. An unbelievably good feeling.

That same week in July 1982 she went to Stoke Mandeville for her six-monthly visit to her consultant. The staff, accustomed to see her shuffling in painfully from the car with the aid of her two sticks, were obviously delighted when she pranced in wearing her high-heeled sandals. Her consultant did a double-take as she made her entry.

'You're admiring my footwork?' she said.

'Would you mind doing another lap of the surgery?' he asked.

Joyce obliged.

'Mm. Let's have a closer look.'

For the first time he was able to note that there was a very definite improvement in her condition in place of the previous steady deterioration. There was evidence of regrowth of nerves.

He said, 'You haven't had physiotherapy since your last examination?'

'No.'

He sensed that something had happened but did not question her. She did not feel like telling him or anyone else in the medical world that she had been to a healer. It was all too precious. She was afraid that this thing could somehow be terminated if people were disbelieving or cynical. So she kept her counsel.

'Whatever treatment you're having,' the consultant said, 'do carry on with it.'

> A totally triumphant week was finished by my going to a party, showing off, and unmindful of the limitations of movement in the foot, falling heavily. The pain was excruciating, and the swelling was alarming. After a long, painful night, when sleep refused to take over, a telephone call to PE resulted in me being taken to Roundstreet House, after I had managed to crawl backwards into the car, because I could not bear the pain of standing on the foot. After treatment, I could bear my weight on the foot for short periods. By the following day, the swelling had reduced drastically. The improvement continues, and a consistent pattern has emerged of nerve pains in the foot and ankle, followed by strong sensations of heat and cold, suppleness of toes, increasing nimbleness in walking, and, best of all, love of life.'

In January 1983 she went back to Stoke Mandeville for the regular check-up. She had made up her mind to tell her consultant that she had been to a healer and that this was what had led to her extraordinary recovery.

By an unhappy chance Dr M was absent and she was examined by a consultant she had not seen before who did not know the whole story. He was pleased and satisfied by what he saw and pronounced her cured. She was told that her treatment was considered a success. They were closing her file and discharging her. Though she could come back at any time if she needed help there was no need for her to continue with the twice-yearly check-ups.

All the staff who had followed her case were delighted. Joyce did not want to spoil their pleasure. She could not bring herself to tell them that in fact she owed her recovery to a healer who had done no more than lay his hands on her.

There had been an unexpected spin-off from Joyce's sessions with the healer. For years Michael had suffered from impaired hearing. It affected his left ear and the deafness was so bad that he always had to sit with his right ear towards the person he was having a conversation with. Michael had not sought any healing for himself. He had sat in the waiting-room while Joyce was receiving healing. He noticed that gradually he was recovering hearing in his right ear. Putting it down to the healing atmosphere at Roundstreet he asked Phil to give him direct healing. By the end of 1982 his hearing was such that even a rather low-voiced person meeting him for the first time never suspected that his hearing was not perfectly normal.

Phil has not discharged Joyce. He feels that there is still work to be done restoring the shattered nerves and building up her well-being. She still continues to see him every two weeks.

When you visit the delightful house in Aldwick and meet this couple for the first time you get the impression that they are almost in a state of shock, but of joyful shock. The two extraordinary happenings which have totally changed their lives are so recent. First, there was the news that Michael had inherited a house from his mother. Then, when they moved into it he had met Phil and this had led to the healing of Joyce. It all gave a new meaning to the word 'synchronicity'.

FREDA EVEREST

Disease: Failure of knee-joints, undiagnosed.

'The doctors and specialists plus two hospitals had not been able to heal it and Phil has. I am ready to accept that.'

Mrs Freda Everest is in her thirties. She was brought up as a member of the Church of England, though she was not at any time an ardent church-goer. She has a son and daughter still of primary-school age. She and her husband divorced towards the end of 1982. Now she lives with the children in a housing estate on the outskirts of Burgess Hill.

Up till November 1982 she worked as transport manager in her husband's business. It was a demanding job and involved a great deal of stress. She had always been an active person with a desire to remain in good physical condition. She was fond of walking and keen on gardening, her particular interest being roses. By 1980 she had started to attend keep-fit classes.

Her knee trouble began on 1 December 1980. She was entering a hall where a function was taking place when her left knee suddenly buckled and gave way. She would have crashed to the ground if she had not been able to grab a nearby chair. There was a sudden stab of severe pain and she found that she was unable to bend her knee.

Her GP prescribed anti-inflammation tablets, but soon the right knee also began to give out. She now found it very difficult and painful to walk. The cause of the condition remained a mystery.

By Christmas of that year her knees were swollen and she could hardly bend them. It was impossible to drive far in the car. While sitting at her desk in the office she'd suffer pain shooting through her legs. The treatment included cortisone injections but this did not seem to be effective and she insisted on having X-rays. They showed 'slight wear' and the beginning of osteoarthritis.

She attended hospital in Haywards Heath for heat treatment and physiotherapy and began to read books about osteoarthritis. As a consequence of her reading she told her GP that she wanted a second opinion. He referred her to an orthopaedic consultant at Cuckfield Hospital. After examining her the consultant said that she would be all right till she was sixty and then full osteoarthritis would probably set in. Meantime, if she had pain he advised her to go to her doctor for pain-killers.

This was hardly a reassuring diagnosis, but she went back to try and live as normal a life as possible. She avoided doing things that would trigger off the knee trouble. She cut her driving down to short journeys, avoided standing in queues, gave up walking and, sadly, curtailed the gardening activities. Unfortunately emotional crises would trigger off pain and by the summer of 1982, with divorce looming up, there was much emotional stress.

It was in August 1982 that a business contact of her husband talked to her about healing. There was a healer in Haywards Heath, but he advised Freda to go to Phil Edwardes, as he had a reputation for being very good with her kind of problem.

Her first appointment was for Friday 27 August. She had just returned from a holiday, the highlight of which had been a visit to a beautiful rose-garden. Her conversation with Phil and the things he told her made a deep impression. Afterwards, when she received healing she had the illusion that she was back in that lovely rose-garden. She felt peaceful, almost asleep, but was conscious enough to have the impression that Phil's hands on her knees were extremely cold. When the healing ended she remained in her dreamy state, had to force herself to get up and walk out of the healing-room. She still felt totally relaxed.

Next day she did something she had not been able to attempt for two years. She drove to Princes Risborough, a journey which took all of two hours. She arrived with no pain at all.

By her second visit a fortnight later she was far less depressed. Phil's talk had influenced her so much that her whole philosophy of life was changed. But that second time, though Phil's hands were warm, she did not think that the healing for her had been strong. Nevertheless, he instructed her: 'Do all the things that you used to do, even if you have not been able to do them lately.'

So she took his advice and started to garden again.

In all she went for three healing sessions, spread over a period of one month. After that last one Phil said he thought that she was now cured and she agreed.

By Christmas 1982 she had almost forgotten about her knee

joints. She was driving, gardening, getting down on the floor to play with the kids. She knew now that if she had a problem she could cope with it. The emotional crises which used to upset her so much left her unscathed. She had even started to redecorate the house with her own hands, clambering up ladders to do the walls and going down on her knees to paint the skirting.

'The doctors and specialists plus two hospitals had not been able to heal it and Phil has. I am ready to accept that.'

CAROLINE ROSE

Disease: Rheumatoid arthritis.

'It's good, that's for sure, a really wonderful feeling, being at peace with the world.'

Caroline is in her late twenties. She is a nice-looking brunette with a vivacious face and very attractive personality. She lives in Walton-on-Thames with her mother and father. But Caroline is independent. Her parents fade into the background and leave her to receive and deal with her visitor.

She wears a longish, very full skirt and fashionable leather boots. She walks with a kind of bouncing walk that is not ungainly. In conversation she prefers a piano stool to the conventional type of chair. She talks in an animated way, using her eyes expressively.

By the age of sixteen she knew that she wanted to be a model. After training at Lucie Clayton's she had a number of offers of work. Her father persuaded her to go back to college. She just had time to take an A-level in English Literature at Wimbledon Common before disease struck.

She was admitted to Roehampton Hospital where the diagnosis indicated that the pains in her joints were due to rheumatic fever, for which there was no cure. At the age of seventeen she was in a ward full of the aged and dying. Her GP decided that it would be better if she were nursed at home.

Just after her eighteenth birthday the pains began to subside, each day there was an improvement. Six months later she was on her way to Australia to convalesce.

After a year out there she had to return home, because of pains in her right hip. She was seen by a rheumatologist and after numerous tests it was confirmed that at the age of nineteen and a half Caroline was suffering from rheumatoid arthritis. The disease was attacking and destroying her hip.

But the disease did not stop there. For the next five years she was in and out of Charing Cross Hospital. Successively she had to have replacement joints put in both her hips and both her knees.

For a year she was all right. Then her right ankle started to play up. The joint was wearing out. Gradually it became more and more distorted. In the end her foot was bent over almost in an L-shape, so that she was virtually putting her weight on the ankle bone.

She suffered incredible pain. Walking was hell. Her range was twenty-five yards. There was some relief when she had her foot up. She was on very strong pain-killers, taking two pain-killers five times a day.

'The next stop was morphine.'

Early in 1980 she again saw the surgeon who had done the operations on her hips and knees. A man not given to showing emotion, he explained simply that replacement ankle joints were not available — not yet anyway. The only thing he could do was 'stiffen' it.

Caroline knew that the progress of rheumatoid arthritis is that the joints become more and more distorted. This is a painful process. When the distortion is finished the joint stiffens in that position, and the pain goes away. She realized that what the surgeon intended to do was to break her ankle joint — 'to mash it about' — and let it set in the new position. She found the idea that she would have absolutely no movement in her ankle whatsoever hard to face. She agreed to go into hospital but she had a strong feeling that it was not right.

The evening before the operation she discharged herself.

Six months later she was back in hospital again. The pain of her ankle had become worse and worse. Again she had the same conviction that what she was doing was not right. Naturally, her doctors wanted her to go through with it. They were only too aware of what she was enduring and they could see no other way she could get relief.

Her surgeon said: 'Your ankle is as bad as any I've seen. It's just going to get worse and worse and you'll have more pain.'

Nevertheless an hour later she again discharged herself.

'I was literally a write-off,' she said of herself at this stage. Agonizing pain in her right ankle, pain in her shoulders, neck and upper back, pain in her hands where the fingers were becoming distorted.

The following Sunday she saw the TV programme *The Medicine Men.* She saw Phil Edwardes healing a woman. After the programme her mother suggested: 'Why don't you go to a healer?'

'It's not logical. No way can anyone mend a bone that's crumbled.'

'What have you got to lose?'

But she would not agree to go.

Her birthday was in January. That was January 1982. Her mother's present was a copy of the book *The Medicine Men,* based on the TV series. She read about Phil Edwardes. She thought: 'Why not try it?'

She rang him up, told him her problem. He said: 'Do come along. We'll give it a try.'

She paid her first visit to Roundstreet House on 2 February.

'As soon as I saw the guy, I sensed there was something about him. He came across as a genuine man.'

Her first sensation was of pins and needles, mostly in her shoulders and ankles. She felt a tingling and heat. She had a warm feeling, a loving feeling. 'It's good, that's for sure, a really wonderful feeling, being at peace with the world.'

Next day she 'did all the shops in Weybridge and that's a lot of shops'. She stopped taking pain-killers. The pain had gone from her ankle.

Then she overdid it. Next time she saw Phil he explained that she had to be patient. When you take a joint out of plaster you don't go crashing about on it, do you? You take it easy, you wait for it to heal.

On that second occasion she felt quite a bit of heat. 'I felt that much better within me. I'd been dragging this old ankle around for such a long time and suddenly this weight was taken off me.'

The third visit was much the same, but on the fourth she was able to drive herself down in the car. After this and subsequent visits she drove herself for miles and miles, enjoying the sense of well-being, of feeling so much better in herself.

Her experience during healing varied. One time, sitting on the stool and looking out through the window, she saw herself running across a field. Another time she felt *three* hands touching her. Out of the corner of her eye she could see Phil's hands on either side of her head, and there was a third hand on the back of her neck. A lot of heat came from this third hand.

For the first six months the heat she felt was on the right side of her shoulder and not the left. One day she commented on this to Phil. Almost at once she got heat on the left side as well. Since then healing has been stronger than ever and she has felt the heat on both sides of her shoulder. After every healing session she feels whacked. She has to sit and relax and then she feels terrific benefit.

As the months went by and she continued to visit Phil the ankle-joint began to straighten out. Under the influence of healing — and healing alone — it was resuming its natural shape.

She had only asked for help with her ankle, relief from the pain. But so much more was happening, more healing was being given to her.

Phil said: 'Now we're looking past the ankle. Let's do something about the muscles in your right leg.'

In March she measured the thigh muscle of her right leg, the one which was always being dragged along. It was one inch smaller in circumference than the left. She measured it again in October. It had expanded by three-quarters of an inch.

Healing was directed also to the area of her upper back, shoulders and neck. During healing she felt her shoulder blade as if it was growing and pushing her shoulders into a better position. That feeling continued even after healing. Since then she has had no further pain in that area. Since the third session her hands too have been getting better and better.

The graph of healing does not show a steady climb. It goes up a bit and then there's a flat patch. Then it goes up again. But there has been no deterioration since 2 February and the progress has always been upwards.

During this time she was receiving no other medical treatment. In June, four and a half months after she had started to have healing, she went back to Charing Cross Hospital for blood tests. She went again in August to see her rheumatologist and enquire about the results.

There was not a lot of difference, he told her. But, he added, the haemoglobin count was up.

On Monday, 2 October, she went to an appointment with her surgeon. She had not been seen by him for eighteen months. When she went in he was sitting at his desk with a number of students round him. He was looking at papers or X-rays or something. He did not pay particular attention as she walked past his desk. Then he glanced up and did a double-take.

He had, of course, expected to see her hobble past with her ankle bent over as he had last seen it. She went on into the cubicle, sat down and took her boot off.

When he came in he asked: 'How's the ankle?'

'It's fine.'

'Has it gone stiff, then?'

If her ankle was giving her less trouble it could only be because it had stiffened in the distorted position — or so one would normally assume.

'I can also rotate it,' she told him. And did so.

He was, to use her word, 'flabbergasted'. His look said it all.

He called his students round, and talked to them in medical terms which went over her head. She understood it was to the effect that with the human body you never know — its inbuilt healing mechanism could produce astonishing results.

Caroline mentioned that she had been going to a healer. He then asked her if she would walk up and down the surgery. She did so with considerable ease.

'Whatever you've been doing,' the surgeon said, 'I suggest that you carry on.'

On her next visit to Phil the healing was as strong as ever. And not long after she was able to go to a disco and enjoy a full evening's dancing.

ERNEST ATKINSON

Disease: Narcolepsy.

'When the band of colour passed the rose became normal again.'

Narcolepsy is an unusual disease. Only one person in 20,000 develops it. In normal people heavy sleep is preceded and followed by a period of light sleep. A narcoleptic goes straight into deep sleep on the instant. It is so sudden that the sufferer may simply fall down on the floor, pavement, field or wherever he is. He literally *falls* asleep, but the sleep may only last for a few seconds. No cure has yet been found by orthodox medicine.

Ernest Atkinson is a bespectacled man of strong and solid build in his middle sixties. He is by profession a chartered engineer and a member of the Institute of Mechanical Engineers. From 1948 to 1973 he worked for an engineering company as their representative for the London and South East area as well as for all overseas trade. The job suited him down to the ground; he was his own master and the ruler of his own destiny. In 1973 they told him that they had a nice little soft number for him as Export Sales Manager. He became a nine till five man. That did not suit him at all and he was glad to retire in 1981.

He has had the misfortune to be widowed twice. He married again in 1982 and lives with his wife in a bungalow on the outskirts of Horsham. He has a small garden, which is essential for Ernie. His great interest is roses and he is Treasurer of the Horsham Horticultural Society.

The first time narcolepsy showed up was thirty years ago. He had taken a party of lads for an outing to Box Hill and in the middle of a game of football he suddenly blacked out and collapsed. At that time he did not know the cause and anyway the disease did not affect him seriously until much later.

In 1980 his second wife had to undergo an operation and she never came out of the anaesthetic. It was the emotional consequences of this tragedy and shock that brought the narcolepsy on in a more acute form. In Ernie's case it was triggered by emotion and could happen suddenly, even during a telephone call. Excitement could bring it on, as well as difficult encounters with people. Nor dared he tell jokes nor watch comics like Morecambe and Wise on television unless he was sitting down. The disease could affect him so swiftly that he would simply fall down. For some time after the death of his wife he dared not drive a car for fear of suddenly falling asleep.

The one thing which was most certain to bring it on was watching football, either live or on the television.

His GP was one of a syndicate of ten doctors in Horsham. When Ernie told him that he was apt to fall suddenly asleep he took it calmly. He remarked that this was quite a common failing. It was only when Ernie saw a television programme on the illness that he realized he could be suffering from narcolepsy.

His GP now took things seriously enough to refer him to a consultant at a hospital in Hooley near Redhill. Ernie realized that the matter was regarded as urgent when he received a prescription from his GP by the first post next morning. The drug prescribed was Dexamphetamin, which prevented him from falling asleep. But it was a 'hard' drug and his doctor was anxious to get him off it as soon as possible.

From then on the practice to which his GP belonged began monitoring research worldwide on the disease of narcolepsy.

Ernie had been present when Phil Edwardes had spoken about healing in Horsham. He thought then that healing could be of help to him with his complaint but decided that he would leave it until he retired. Now the time had come. His GP was all in favour of him going to a healer; he said that it could do no harm and he would be very interested in monitoring the result.

He first went to Phil Edwardes in November 1981. Phil had never heard of narcolepsy; all he could do, he said, was give Ernie healing and see what happened.

To Ernie's surprise when they went into the healing-room Phil placed on the window-sill in front of him a vase with a single rose in it. He told Ernie to concentrate on the rose and think of nothing else. Ernie had no problem in relaxing, he had taken up yoga some time ago. His only fear was that he'd topple off the stool, but during healing he had no inclination to fall asleep. What was happening was far too interesting.

While Phil was passing his hands over his shoulders and head he noticed a wave of colour coming diagonally across his field of vision. 'It came in golden bands of a rich orange-reddish almost flame-like colour. As it passed over the rose it brought out the detail of the flower in an exceptional three-dimensional way. When the band of colour passed the rose became normal again. Then another band came and the same effect was repeated.'

The bands of colour had at first been narrow but as the healing progressed they became wider. He felt something going on behind his right eye, which is the 'lazy' eye. He could not find words to describe what it was like: 'I had a most peculiar sensation.'

He went for healing again a week later. This time there was no rose on the window-sill in front of him but once again he saw those bands of colour moving across. He also had the same peculiar sensation that 'something was going on behind each eye from outside the left and right side of my head.'

After this second visit he decided to monitor his improvement. His grandson came round to the house to tell him that he was playing football on a nearby recreation ground. Would Grandad like to come and watch? Watching a kid he loved play football would be as tough a test as any he could devise. He went along to the ground and was soon running up and down the touchline urging the lad on. It was the first time he had watched football for twenty years: 'I just could not believe it was taking place.'

Early on in the healing programme he was able to come off the drug Dexamphetamin. As time went on he found he could face with confidence more and more situations which previously would have brought on an attack. He was able to reduce the frequency of his visits to Roundstreet from once a week to once a month and at the end of 1982 was still attending regularly. Even now the healing is still accompanied by those characteristic bands of colour.

His GP was pleased when Ernie was able to dispense with the drug and very interested in the progress of his recovery. The practice to which the doctor belongs continued their worldwide search for a cure for narcolepsy.

MALCOLM LAIRD

Disease: Agoraphobia.

'An up-and-coming disease.'

Agoraphobia is usually described as a dread of open places but it can also include a dread of such places as supermarkets and railway stations. In fact agoraphobia overlaps in many ways with claustrophobia, a dread of enclosed places. Malcolm Laird, who suffers from agoraphobia, says it is 'an up-and-coming disease'; many young people are starting to get one or other of these phobias. The consequences are drastic. Travelling by car is a problem. After six or seven miles he begins to feel desperate. Shops and busy streets are intolerable. Only the home base is secure.

In the late 1960s Malcolm was a flight inspector with H.S.A. Ltd. To the normal pressure of his work was added that of finding a home for himself and his wife to live in. The only house they could find within their means was an old and dilapidated bungalow near Billingshurst. The Building Society gave him a mortgage on condition that he restored and redecorated it, got water and electricity laid on all within one year. During that year Malcolm and his wife also had his grandmother living with them.

Malcolm met the deadline but the pressure on him had been too much. In 1972 he had a nervous breakdown. It left him with agoraphobia and a complaint known as tinnitus, which is a constant and maddening ringing in the ear. For a time it was impossible to go out of the house.

Doctors have been unable to help him. He has tried acupuncturists, psychologists and psychiatrists to no avail. It has become impossible for him and his wife ever to take a holiday. The limit of his range is six or seven miles. Within that area he has found a job at Wisborough Green, working for a firm which restores vintage Rolls-Royce and Bentley cars.

In 1982 he decided to try healing and went to Phil Edwardes eight or nine times. At the end of that time he and Phil agreed that this treatment was not really helping his nervous condition, the agoraphobia. The tinnitus, however, was helped. Whereas the ringing in his right ear used to be continuous it is now only intermittent.

Malcolm is not unresponsive to healing and though it had not helped his agoraphobia he still believed in it. When he developed pains in his back and across his chest — possibly the result of lying under a Rolls-Royce for too long — he went back to Phil. The pains were healed in one session.

His wife had 'a problem with her tummy'. Malcolm took her to see Phil. Under healing she felt a rippling sensation that went right in where the trouble was and gave a feeling of warmth. Although she was not completely cured, her trouble was very much eased.

Malcolm Laird's case is an example of where healing failed. None the less he says, 'I'd go to another healer rather than a doctor.'

NOREEN, MICHAEL AND CAROLINE IRVING-SWIFT

Diseases: Spine complications after double laminectomy;
sciatica;
verrucas and warts.

'. . . felt a presence coming up behind me almost as if the air was vibrating . . .'

The Irving-Swifts live in a Georgian house surrounded by an extensive garden and set in the Sussex countryside.

Michael spent the greater part of his life in the Esso oil company, as a senior executive during his later years with them. He has the realistic and practical attitude that you would expect from one who has worked in such a competitive and commercially-orientated business. This does not mean that he is materialistic. He believes in God, but is not a regular church-goer.

Noreen his wife was brought up in India, where her family on the paternal side had worked for several generations. Her father also was an oil man. Noreen in her youth was a keen horsewoman and played a lot of squash and tennis.

Caroline their daughter is aged twenty-four. She lives in London and is the manageress of a wine bar in the City, a very demanding and stressful job.

Mother, father and daughter have all been to Phil Edwardes for healing.

When Noreen was sixteen she decided to ride a high-spirited stallion, which was in fact a racehorse. It bolted with her, a stirrup broke, she fell off and was dragged by one leg. She was lucky to escape without apparent serious injury, but the mishap led to back problems during the ensuing years. Doctors she consulted encouraged her by telling her that tall and thin people were liable to have back trouble and she'd just got to live with it.

By the 1970s these problems became acute. As she was not getting much joy from the orthodox doctors she went for treatment first to an osteopath and then a chiropractor. However, it became increasingly evident that if she did not have an operation she would probably spend the rest of her life in a wheelchair. It seemed almost incidental when at about this time her foot was stood on by a pony and her toe badly damaged. In 1976 she consulted a neurosurgeon, a member of the Royal College of Surgeons, about her back. He operated on her in the Hurstwood Hospital near Haywards Heath. The operation was 'a double laminectomy' — removing worn-out discs which are impinging on the spinal cord and causing pain.

In the years following this operation Noreen suffered pain which became progressively less bearable. She was reluctant to go back to her surgeon because she could not face the thought of another operation like the first one. She began seeing an osteopath in Horsham. This treatment relieved the pain for a time but it always returned.

Christmas 1980 was approaching. The family were coming home and a number of house guests had been invited. It was now that Noreen suffered her worst experience. All the extra effort involved in the preparations brought on acute pain. She became so ill that Michael thought, as he put it, 'that she was reaching the end of her tether'.

She came through but the whole thing gave him a bad scare.

He decided to accept the terms for early retirement which were then being offered by his company. After 1 April, the date of retirement, life became easier for Noreen as he was able to take on many of her tasks. But the condition of her back did not improve. Standing up after being seated was agonizing. She could only struggle upstairs by hauling on the banisters. On one occasion she hauled so hard that she actually broke them. Getting up in the morning was 'a hassle'; she had to start the day by crawling around the bedroom on all fours to loosen up.

Michael and Noreen had heard about Phil Edwardes from friends. Noreen was ready to try healing. She felt that she had come to the end of the line with orthodox medicine. An appointment was made for 5 October 1982.

On this first visit she was driven over by Caroline. For some reason she believed that the healing lasted for only four minutes. She felt it as both heat and vibration. When Phil came round from behind her she saw that his face was grey as if a lot of energy had been drawn from him.

He told her to stand up. To her own astonishment she found herself standing up erect for the first time in years. It felt 'as if someone had undone something'. She walked out of the healing-room free of pain. Though she subsequently had twinges the old pain did not return.

On the next visit she felt even the twinges being removed and at the same time heat on her head, shoulders, spine and toes. Nine days later she told Phil about her toe that had been stepped on by the pony. So he gave her healing for the toe as well. Within a week it had grown so much better that for the first time in six years she was able to wear fashionable shoes without discomfort.

Healing was strong for her and on her fourth visit even before Phil moved from his chair she 'felt a presence coming up behind me, almost as if the air was vibrating'.

By the end of November she seemed to be completely cured. Indeed, meeting her at the end of that month one could not imagine that so recently she had been in such pain. Her whole manner was relaxed, her way of walking elegant and graceful and her posture when seated totally relaxed. The final proof was the serenity and tranquillity of her features.

In his concern for Noreen, Michael had ignored his own problem. He had a pinched sciatic nerve and a lot of pain in the left leg. It was bad enough to force him to read books standing upright. In bed at night he was in such discomfort that he could not sleep. Hard-bitten oil-man though he was he had seen what Phil had done for Noreen. Perhaps there would be some healing for him?

As it turned out he did not benefit in the same way as his wife. He felt relaxed and was quite moved emotionally. There was a sensation of heat in his whole spine. It took four or five sessions before there was any real improvement, and even then it did not last. By the turn of the year he was back to square one. At Phil's suggestion he also went to see an osteopath and the two treatments in conjunction led to a great improvement. Healing alone was not enough to cure Michael's back but he still remains 'quite a disciple of healing'. He has persuaded several of his friends to go to Phil and they have all benefited.

Caroline had suffered from a distressing complaint since the age of thirteen. She had verrucas on her feet. This was a tiresome thing for a young girl to endure as verrucas are contagious and one has to be careful about bathmats, towels and so on. But at least these blemishes don't show. The same could not be said of the wart she developed on her thumb during 1982. It was unsightly and a constant embarrassment to someone in her job. All in all she was in an extremely nervy state, under great pressure in her work and absolutely fed up with life. The specialists to whom she was sent by her GP treated her with acid, laser beams and incision with the knife, but the verrucas and wart refused to budge. Her GP was baffled. She was not sure whether he was being serious when he said, 'The only thing you can do is go to a healer.'

So, on 5 October Caroline went along to have healing herself. She came out from the experience 'shattered', to use her mother's description. During the next week the verrucas hurt a lot but within two weeks they disappeared altogether. The wart felt as if it was being pulled out, and it had simply disappeared within a week. By her third visit on 12 November her hand and her feet were free from blemishes and they have remained that way. Moreover she was already facing life differently. Phil had got her thinking positively and everything had changed for the better.

So, here we have a mother, father and daughter who all went to Phil Edwardes and during the short period between the beginning of October and the end of December had seen their lives completely change.

SYD BYFORD

Disease: Cancer.

'I was going through a tunnel and at the end were people I knew who had died.'

Syd works in the administrative department of a borough in south-east London. In his free time he does first-aid work and is a member of St John's Ambulance. He is also an officer in the Boys' Brigade and runs a bugle band.

From early childhood he has been endowed with an abnormal perceptiveness. He was often able to see people who were invisible to others. As a small boy this frequently got him into trouble. There was one occasion when he was, apparently, alone with his mother in the house. She asked him to lay the table. He laid four places, including the two extra visitors he could see. He was locked in a cupboard as a punishment. That taught him to be reticent about what he saw but he still has this extraperceptive sight.

In 1978 he had a tumour on the prostate gland. In hospital the diagnosis was that 90 per cent of the gland was diseased. He was given radiotherapy. He was in considerable pain and it was agony to walk. At this time a friend of his was going down to see Phil Edwardes. Syd went along, just for the ride. But in the end he went in for healing too.

The effect was astonishing. He felt 'as if I was going through a tunnel and at the other end were people I knew who had died'. He saw his mother who had recently died, and also his father, who had died way back in 1945 at the age of thirty-five. Phil's hands felt almost hot enough to burn him. The healing went straight to the affected part.

During healing sessions at Roundstreet he saw many other people invisible to others. One was an old lady dressed in nineteenth-century costume sitting out in the garden. He went out and had a talk with her. She had been the owner of Roundstreet House long ago. 'It is good, what is going on here,' she told him.

When in due course he went into Guy's Hospital for the operation it was found that the gland was significantly less cancerous than had previously been diagnosed. It was 'scraped off and generally cleaned up'.

Syd believes in using healing as a complement to orthodox medical treatment. Healing before the operation appeared to alleviate the condition and healing afterwards speeded his recovery. He went on attending the hospital for treatment over the same period as he was having healing. He now appears to be in fine shape.

Syd confides reluctantly that he has himself the healing power: 'One hand finds the trouble spot, the other heals it.' But Syd does not want to be set up as a healer, at least not overtly. He prefers to heal anonymously. He has had some evidence that strangers towards whom he directed healing in public places have felt a sudden easement. His first-aid work enables him to do this more directly. He can pretend to apply the standard methods to the sick or injured but in fact he is giving them healing. He also finds that he is good at absent healing. Indeed he prefers to do it in this way because then he can be more anonymous, less personally involved with the subject.

Syd raised this point: How many healers are there going around healing people anonymously, and the people don't even realize it's happening?

MARGARET BANNISTER

Disease: Eczema.

'I was just tearing my skin apart. I could understand why people commit suicide.'

Margaret is a young mother in her early thirties. Her first child James is just one year old. Her husband is an airline pilot with British Airways. He now flies Concorde on the London-New York route. That means he is absent a lot — one week at home followed by one week away. They live just outside Chobham in one of the oldest houses in the village.

Margaret had eczema when she was twelve but it cleared up

and she thought she had seen the last of it. After leaving school she took a secretarial job in an advertising agency and then, in 1976, became a stewardess with British Airways.

In those days she was flying in VC10s to destinations in North Africa and Ethiopia. The variety and the chance to see faraway places was stimulating but alongside the glamour there were serious drawbacks. The hours were very irregular, made worse by the difference in time between one country and another. During trips she never got much sleep, was always eating the wrong food, partaking of too much drink. And often there was jet-lag. At the end of a flight the crew would board a minibus, dog-tired, to be driven to some impersonal hotel. Inevitably they would have a few drinks, get a second wind and put off the much-needed sleep.

The crew used to stay together for seven or eight days and it was on one of these trips that she met the pilot who was to become her husband. They fell in love and by the end of that tour had decided to get married.

After the wedding Margaret went on flying, though it would only be by good luck if she found herself in the same crew as Mark. Being married added new stresses to her way of life. It was difficult to combine flying with running and enjoying the kind of life a young couple have the right to expect.

The stress began to show in the autumn of 1979 when her eczema started to come back. Patches of it broke out on various parts of her body. She was sent by British Airways to see various doctors but they could not check the spread of the disease. When she became pregnant the eczema became very bad indeed. Soon her body was covered with it.

At the end of 1979 British Airways were cutting down on staff. There was a severance scheme which offered attractively generous terms to those who wished to quit. The airline's own doctors advised her to accept severance and give up flying. She knew she had no alternative. In her condition flying was out of the question.

So long as the eczema was on the concealed part of her body she could lead a fairly normal life, but when it spread to her hands and then her face she found it distressing to appear in public. People in shops would glance at her face and then exclaim in horror. The irritation was intolerable and she had no respite from it, it was there twenty-four hours a day.

'I was just tearing my skin apart. I could understand why people commit suicide.'

Severed from British Airways she now came under her GP in Woking. He told her that she was the worst case of eczema in his experience. There was not a clear patch on her body on which you could have stuck a pin. Her doctor referred her to a dermatologist in the area. The dermatologist prescribed steroids which did suppress the excema a bit. Sometimes her face would clear completely, only to be covered by the eczema once more.

She underwent allergy tests. It was found that she was allergic to dairy produce, household dust and animals. She avoided all these but the eczema did not improve. Her doctors could not account for it.

Without abandoning her GP and dermatologist she tried other forms of medicine — acupuncture, naturopathy, hypnotherapy and two different homoeopaths. None of their treatments had any significant effect on her condition.

When her son was born things improved. Her spirits rose and she thought that now she had turned the corner. But no. When James was three months old the disease came back worse than ever. She went into post-natal depression. It was a black and terrible time. Her doctors were giving her stronger and stronger steroids and different creams to rub on. Cortisone was tried. The pills had the effect of making her walk round in a dream, which is no good when you have a baby to look after.

One day in despair she rang her mother: 'Mum, I just can't cope any more.'

Naturally her mother came at once. She had heard her brother talking about Phil Edwardes. She suggested that Margaret should go and see the healer. Margaret thought it was worth a try and rang up to fix an appointment.

On her first visit, it was 31 August 1982, she simply felt tranquil during healing and relaxed in a way she had never done before. Driving back home she thought, 'Well, I *can* cope with this.'

After two or three visits at intervals of one week a definite improvement was noticeable. Her husband came home from a trip one day and said, 'Gosh, your face is looking better!'

On the way home after that third visit she had thrown all her pills and potions out of the car window. She has not taken any since.

By the fourth visit the eczema had almost cleared from the top half of her body including her face. By the fourth the lower part was clearing up. The chats she had with Phil before healing made a big difference to her: 'He talked to me as doctors never do.' As a result of those chats and the healing which followed them her attitude to life was changing. Phil explained that something might be happening inside her which was having an effect on the condition of her skin. Understanding this helped her.

During healing one day she had confirmation that something was happening inside her. Sitting on the stool she felt so faint that she nearly fell off. Phil had to sit her down and fetch her a glass of water. It was some time before she was ready to start the drive home. Later Phil told her that the healing then had been particularly strong. In the next few days her skin was worse, 'as if something was coming out', and thereafter the improvement continued even more rapidly.

By the end of November she had paid twelve visits to Roundstreet over a period of three months. All that remained of the eczema were a couple of minor patches on her ankles and wrists. Her face had been unblemished for a couple of months. In addition she had lost her allergies. One day, tempted by a platter of cheese, she had impulsively decided to indulge herself. Before healing that would have immediately have caused her face to 'come up'. This time it had no effect. That night, unheard of luxury, she went to bed with a cup of Horlicks. 'Now,' she says, 'I can eat the lot.'

During this period she has had no treatment other than Phil Edwardes' healing. And his healing has consisted simply of laying his hands on her head and shoulders.

In January 1983 Margaret went to her doctor for a check-up. She had decided to tell him the true reason for her astonishing recovery: 'He's a super chap and I like him very much.'

He examined her and confirmed with pleasure and satisfaction that she was virtually cured.

'Would you like to know why?' she asked him.

'The pills presumably proved effective.'

'I stopped taking them months ago. No, the real reason is that I have been going to a healer.'

The effect of the announcement was disappointing.

'How interesting,' he said.

'What do you think about it?'

'I can't comment. If you think it's doing you good, then fine.'

She could tell from his tone that he considered it had been a case of mind over matter and that if she had shown the same faith in his pills they would have cured her. She did not insist. She knows the true reason for her cure, and has so much confidence in the effectiveness of healing that she has persuaded a friend of hers who has equally bad eczema to go to Phil for treatment.

The sinus trouble from which she suffers has not so far been cured, but after the most recent visit she 'streamed and streamed'. She will continue to go for healing in the hope that this means the sinuses will be the next thing to be healed.

GEORGE DOBSON

Disease: Ulcers on the legs.

'Just get me out of the pain and you've done a deal.'

George is about sixty-four. He is a solidly-built, tallish man with greying hair, a moustache and a pair of twinkling eyes. He walks fairly normally with only the slightest suggestion of a hobble. When he sits down he is relaxed and free from pain.

He is married and has two daughters. He has spent most of his life in the building trade, often up and down scaffolding. A few years ago one of his daughters pointed out that he was not going to be able to go on in the building trade much longer and persuaded him to set up a travel business with her in London. So, George would spend the week in Worthing on his building business and go up to London at the weekend to see to the travel office. The London enterprise was successful, so he decided to open a second office in Worthing. He bought a shop there, but the planning authority wanted it to go on being some kind of retail business. George's wife had some experience in catering. Thanks to his experience in the building trade he converted the shop into a tea-room and restaurant, with a neat little office at the back. The Worthing end of the business is now as flourishing as the London end.

Back in 1964, when he was forty-five, he was suffering from varicose veins, and he had a hernia too. He went into Princess Beatrice's Hospital in London. The specialist told him he'd have to have three separate operations — one for the hernia, one on the right leg and one on the left. That was going to mean at least six weeks off work.

The operation on the hernia went off all right. So did the one on the right leg — so it seemed. But when they put the cicatrine powder on his left leg it was found that he was allergic to it. Instead of strengthening his skin the powder was eroding it away. His leg was soon in a terrible condition. The hospital doctors told him they could not do the operation on his left leg. Physiotherapy was prescribed.

He began to go for physiotherapy five times a week. In spite of it the ulcerations on his leg were not healing. They got bigger and bigger. He had a wife and two kids to support and he was losing all this time away from work and it wasn't doing him any good at all. So he stopped going for physiotherapy and continued putting the ointment, zinc plus castor oil, on himself.

He carried on for ten years, still in the building trade. In 1974 two serious ulcers developed on his left leg. They were raw and nasty, eating the flesh through almost to the bone. Two years later ulceration developed on his right leg also.

He went to see his GP, one of a group practice of four in Worthing. Rightly or wrongly he got the impression that his GP did not feel there was much he could do for him and his leg ulcers. He sent him for treatment to his nurse. In the period of twelve months George saw his doctor only once.

He explained: 'His nurse does them (ulcerated legs) all day and every day. It's the bulk of her work.'

He liked Nurse, got on well with her. And the other patients in the waiting room enjoyed his jokes. Nurse gave him plenty of treatment, put on the ointments, wrapped his legs in bandages — the usual things. But there was no improvement. His legs were getting worse.

Now, a man in the building trade needs his legs. And George's legs were failing. 'Instead of going up the scaffolding myself I was having to tell other blokes to go up and that wasn't any good.'

By early 1980 things had got very bad. He couldn't walk far before he was looking for a seat. He could not sleep at night. Whenever his legs were in a horizontal position they gave him gyp. He used to dangle a leg out of bed onto the floor to get some sleep. As soon as he fell asleep the leg would climb into the bed again. The shooting pains would start up and wake him. He'd get up to go downstairs and then wonder if he could make it to the top of the stairs. He'd struggle down the stairs sideways with the help of the banisters. Pain-killers would help him through the night, sitting upright in an armchair. He was becoming more and more dependent on pain-killers.

The pain in his legs was making him walk in an awkward way. This caused them to deteriorate further. They had become like stumps. 'To go to the surgery I had to psych myself up and when I got there I'd be on my knees.'

So it was back to the doctor. Then on to the nurse. The usual treatment — ointment and bandages. But no betterment.

George's wife was suffering from what seemed to be a trapped nerve in her back. The pain had worked up through her neck and things had got so bad that she could not open her jaws, she could not eat. Orthodox medicine appeared to be unable to help. George decided to bypass his GP. He took his wife to see an osteopath.

The osteopath discovered that the cause of the trouble was a nerve in her elbow. It caused her to tense her arm, and the paralysis spread progressively to her neck and finally to her jaw. A course of treatment put her right, but the trouble came back later.

Early in 1980 George saw the programme *The Medicine Men* on ITV. He says that he saw Phil Edwardes curing a man's legs. (Phil Edwardes did appear in that programme but he was *not* curing a man's legs; he was curing a woman's back.) George forgot Phil's name, but he remembered that a Mr Tester had also appeared in the programme, and that he lived at Haywards Heath.

He wanted now to take his wife to a healer. He wrote a letter and addressed it:

> Mr Tester
> Healer
> Somewhere in Haywards Heath

He posted it on Thursday. He got the reply next Saturday morning.

Mr Tester said that his wife did not need to come to see him; the healing would be by communication. George was disappointed.

That weekend his wife was bad, she had a lot of pain and was confined to bed. George went up to London as was his wont. He telephoned her several times to ask how she was. She gave him evasive answers.

When he got back home on Sunday night he found her up, pottering about and doing little chores — she told him that she had been afraid to say anything on the phone in case it turned out to be only temporary. When she'd got up on Sunday morning the pain had gone. She has not had it since.

George decided he wanted to go to a healer, but he didn't want to go to Tester. He wanted his own man and he wanted to be *seen* by someone. He remembered that there had been another healer on the programme. He rang up TV South. They told him it had been an Anglia programme, advised him to try Norwich. He rang Norwich. All they would tell him was that the healer lived in Sussex and was called Edwardes. With an *e*.

There were only two Edwardes in the phone book. The first number he called he struck lucky.

George went to Nurse for his usual treatment on Wednesday morning and on Wednesday afternoon he paid his first visit to Phil.

'Just get me out of the pain,' he told Phil, 'and you've done a deal.'

When Phil put his hands over George's head on this first visit he felt a vibration under his scalp. It was like a mild electric shock.

The second time, when Phil's hands touched his shoulders they began to twitch. It was only after this that the feeling went down to his legs. When the healing hands went to his legs — barely touching them, if at all — the sensation was hard to describe. It was as though the skin inside was moving up and down against the skin outside.

By the third visit the pain had gone from his knees. He was sleeping at night and feeling a lot better. In fact the ulcer in his right leg, the big one, was beginning to heal.

As healing progressed during the next six months he felt it

differently. Now, when Phil stood up the healing went straight to his legs. Phil touched his head and George felt it in his legs. As soon as Phil's hands touched his legs they began to tremble and jerk. It was as if the vibrations in Phil's hands were echoed in his leg. Again it was like a mild electric shock, sometimes little stabs like electric current under the skin.

Meanwhile George was still going regularly to see Nurse. He'd see her on the Wednesday morning and Phil on the Wednesday afternoon. She was kind and helpful and he enjoyed the treatment. Maybe it was a belt and braces attitude but he is not the sort of man who'd want to appear ungrateful to someone who had sincerely tried to help him. Of about eighteen people attending the surgery he was the only one who was getting better. He had told Nurse that he was going to a healer and being greatly helped by him. She was sceptical. At about that time, July or August, she had started using a new spray and she assured him, 'It's my new spray that's curing your leg, Mr Dobson.' Was it the new spray that was really causing his ulcers to close up and new skin to start forming over what had been raw, seeping wounds? George began to wonder.

In late August and early September 1982 there was about a month during which he was unable to see Phil. First George was away and then Phil was away — on his first holiday for ten years. During Phil's absence George still saw Nurse regularly and was treated with the new spray. Yet his ulcers began to deteriorate. They became raw again and started to ooze. By the time Phil returned they were really bad. Almost back to square one.

As soon as the healing sessions were resumed the ulcers showed immediate signs of improvement. Within a couple of weeks the skin had re-formed to cover the ugly sore on the right leg and the left leg was mending fast. This convinced George that it was Phil Edwardes' healing which was keeping his leg ulcers under control. But he'll go on seeing Nurse on Wednesday mornings. He sees no reason not to combine orthodox medical treatment with collateral healing.

NICOLE BRIGDEN

Disease: Injured knee.

'In three seconds the aircraft dropped 500 feet then rose 1200.'

Mrs Nicole Brigden is aged twenty-four and lives with her husband, Steve, in a village near Lewes. She is an attractive brunette with expressive hands and quick, agile movements. They were married a couple of years ago and decided that rather than start a family they would each go on with their own jobs for the time being. Steve works for the Southern Publishing Company where he is responsible for special projects. He is practical with his hands and did most of the internal work on their bungalow.

Nicole left school at the age of eighteen with three A-levels and then took a secretarial course. Her first two jobs made her realize that she was not an office person. She applied to all the airlines and eventually was given a job as an air stewardess by British Island Airways. This company operates charter flights out of Gatwick to all European destinations, which does not involve Nicole in being away for long periods; she has six days on and two off.

On 18 July 1982 she was on a flight to Alicante in Spain. The outward journey passed without incident and the aircraft, a BAC 111, remained at Alicante for an hour and a half before starting the return journey. The plane was stocked up, the passengers boarded and they took off.

About forty-five minutes out Nicole and the two other girls were serving tea and coffee to the passengers. She felt the aircraft give a jolt and glanced at the seat-belt sign to see if the Captain had switched it on, but he hadn't. Some instinct made her stoop to put the two hot jugs down on the floor. While she was squatting the BAC 111 hit the turbulence. Later she learnt from the report on the incident that in less than three seconds it had dropped 500 feet and then risen 1200 feet. All she knew was that she had hit the roof of the cabin. For an instant, time was suspended. Looking along the cabin she could see that everything loose was up in the air — handbags, cups, books, cigarettes. Then she was back on the floor again between the rows of seats.

She at first felt no pain, but when she looked down she saw that her right leg was bent out sideways in an L shape; it had got caught between the metal supports of a seat when the aircraft dropped. She was the senior stewardess, so her first thought was for the passengers. She got herself up and supporting her weight on the seats dragged herself forward, checking the occupants of the seats.

After about three minutes she was struck by excruciating pain and became incapable of doing any more. Fortunately there was a row of three empty seats and she was laid out on these for the rest of the flight to Gatwick. The ambulance was waiting. Her leg was put in a pneumatic splint and she was taken to Redhill Hospital. There her head, chest and leg were X-rayed. They were more concerned about her head than her leg; that was because in such an accident there is always danger of concussion or spinal injury. Surprisingly no such injuries showed up on the X-ray and the verdict was that her leg was just twisted. She was advised to sleep it off. Steve came to fetch her in the Datsun estate car. By the time they got home at 1 a.m. her knee had stiffened up and she was unable to walk.

Next day, Monday, she went to see her GP. 'We have very good doctors,' she says, 'and the NHS gives us an excellent service.' Her GP felt it was serious enough to refer her to an orthopaedic surgeon at the Royal Sussex in Brighton. When she saw the latter the following Friday he at once decided that the trouble was in her ligaments. He told her that he was going to do an arthroscopy while she was under general anaesthetic. In the event she was in the operating theatre for a couple of hours and when she recovered consciousness her leg was in plaster from toe to thigh. The knee was very painful. She had broken, she learnt, the medial and the post-cruciate ligaments.

She came home on 6 August still in the same plaster. When she saw the surgeon three weeks later it was taken off, the stitches were removed and she got a walking plaster. Her surgeon was very pleased with the outcome of the operation and made an appointment to see her on 7 October. Only after that visit was she started on physiotherapy. That meant going every weekday to Lewes Hospital.

Five weeks later, about the middle of November, she was

having a lot of pain. She saw her surgeon on 11 November and he decided to manipulate her knee under anaesthetic and arranged for her to come into hospital on 11 December. In the end this operation was done by his 'locum' on 7 January, by which time she was getting 'a bit cheesed off'. Her mother, waiting outside the room where the manipulation was done, heard her scream under the anaesthetic. The locum, endeavouring to move the knee through 90°, had heard it crack and grate so he decided to stop at 60°.

In the days following the manipulation she began to sink into depression. She had been told to bend her knee in order to keep it free and moving, at least through 60°, but every time she did this the pain was so intense that it made her scream. Four months had passed since the accident. She was beginning to abandon hope that she'd ever be able to go back to her job and was afraid that she would have a limp for the rest of her life. She was still using two sticks to walk.

One day, in the depths of gloom, she confided her fears to her mother.

'Why don't you try healing?' her mother suggested. She herself had been to Phil Edwardes a few years ago and her spinal trouble had been greatly helped. 'You've got nothing to lose by going to see Mr Edwardes.'

Nicole was ready to give it a chance but Steve was sceptical; he suspected that healers were quacks, but he agreed that she should go for one treatment and see what happened.

Her first visit was on 21 January 1983. During the healing Phil placed his hand over her knee, not touching it. She felt strong heat and within the knee a sensation as if he was touching it. When he put his thumb over the bad spot she felt a stab of pain — sharp but not unbearable.

After the first visit the pain did not go away but the heat she had felt during healing persisted. When other people touched her knee they felt this heat. Nicole herself felt well and, for the first time in many months, cheerful. Steve saw the difference in her and urged her to go for healing at least six times. She was happy to do so but she went on with the regular physiotherapy. She had told Phil that she did not want to burn her boats and he agreed about this — though he warned her not to go overboard on it. In fact, all the physiotherapy consisted of at this time was exercise.

On the second visit a week later there was no improvement in movement but she felt better. There was some sensation of pain but not so intense. On the third the amount of pain was tiny and her leg had slightly more movement.

On 4 February she was again seen by her surgeon at the Royal Sussex. He said that he wanted to do another manipulation – on 18 February.

Before that date she paid two more visits to Roundstreet.

When she went in for the manipulation her surgeon found her so improved that, she said, 'he could not believe it'. He gave her the manipulation and as usual she went on to physiotherapy for the usual follow-up treatment. 'They did all their usual bits, but I just got up and walked out to the car. I felt no pain at all.'

From then on she did not look back. In all she had eight treatments from Phil and she just got better and better.

She was due to see her orthopaedic surgeon on 4 March. When she walked in, she said, he was amazed. He was extremely pleased at her improvement but all the same she felt it better not to say anything about the healing.

'What are you going to do now?' he asked her.

'I'm going to try and get my old job back as air-stewardess.'

From his expression she guessed that he'd never believed that she would recover enough to go back to such an exacting job.

When she went to British Island Airways to ask for her old job she was given a medical by the company's doctors and pronounced fit. Soon afterwards she was again flying as a stewardess.

'If I hadn't gone to Mr Edwardes,' she says, 'I would not be back at work and I'd be walking with a limp. Five months of ordinary treatment had not cured me and two months of healing put me right. I only wish I had gone to him sooner.'

Nicole is sure that the healing process is still going on. Often when she sits down, even on a flight, she feels that same sensation of heat in her knee, though when she touches it the skin temperature is normal. Another benefit of healing is that the long scar on her leg has become almost invisible, rather an important point for a young tennis player who is sensitive about her appearance.

VALERIE MARTIN

Disease: Damaged coccyx, lumps in the breast.

'. . . an extraordinary unfolding and flowering of spirit. Why?'

Valerie and her husband live in a period cottage along a leafy Sussex lane. They have a daughter aged twenty-eight and a son in the Royal Navy who celebrated his twenty-first birthday dodging Exocets out in the Falklands.

Valerie was born in India and spent the first seven years of her life in that country. Her father was an administrator in the Indian Civil Service. Her mother was an accomplished pianist and from her Valerie had inherited a love of music. She also had an artistic talent and in her student days attended classes at Heatherley Art School. Though she had the gift of getting a likeness she was not really successful at portraiture and concentrated mainly on wood engraving. After she married and started a family she gave up art. She was to return to it later in a totally unforeseen way.

One day about the time of her son's first birthday she sat down very hard on the arm of a wooden chair and damaged her coccyx. The trouble lay dormant until early in 1981 when it declared itself in a very acute form. Rest lying flat on her back brought no relief so she tried an osteopath. This only made things worse and the pain increased to screaming intensity.

What made all this harder to bear was that her son was now a cadet at the Royal Naval College in Dartmouth and was due to take part in an important ceremonial parade. She simply had to be there, even though it was a couple of hundred miles away.

She knew about Phil Edwardes because her husband had been to see him about his back trouble, so Valerie made an appointment for herself. She got a friend to drive her to Roundstreet. It was an agonizing journey.

Her diary records her impressions of the first healing session: 'An extraordinary unfolding and flowering of spirit. Why?'

After her second visit she wrote, 'Layers and layers of consciousness being peeled off — what? Getting down to the hidden core, the essence of me.'

After two healings the condition of her spine was so improved that she was able to face driving herself all the way down to Cornwall.

A second problem had been making itself felt for some time. A lump the size of a hazel nut had developed in her breast. There were also two smaller ones. The largest was now apparent when she was wearing a tight sweater. She was reluctant to have it examined by her doctors, so instead of going to her gynaecologist she went to Phil Edwardes. During the next months, while she was going to Roundstreet but receiving no other treatment, the lumps gradually went away.

In May 1981 she went at last to her gynaecologist for a regular check-up. He prodded around and gave his verdict: 'Yes, you did have a lump there. But it's gone now.' He was very interested and somewhat mystified, but she did not tell him that she had been having healing. 'There's a great improvement generally since last time I saw you,' he commented. 'You look quite different.'

In fact an extraordinary thing had happened. Her metabolism had changed and she was in many respects as youthful physically as before she had her first baby. One visible piece of evidence was her waist which had diminished from twenty-eight inches to twenty-two. She had to get rid of most of her wardrobe and buy new clothes. And she had *not* been on a slimming diet. This seemed to be an outcome of the healing. There were other consequences too. She felt such a marked increase in vitality that she began to have daily workouts and could go through a five-hour session at a dance workshop with no sense of fatigue at the end.

Indeed someone meeting her today and trying to guess her age would be at least a decade out. She has the figure and looks of a much younger woman.

After one healing — she was continuing to pay regular visits to Roundstreet — Phil told her that he thought she ought to go and see her gynaecologist again. He did not know why but he sensed that there was something wrong and that a 'second opinion' would be advisable. She did as he suggested. The doctor examined her and then said, a little ominously, 'I think we'd better have you in.'

Before going into hospital she went to see Phil again. During healing on that occasion she felt 'as if a laser beam was going into my tummy right to the spot'.

She duly went into hospital and had the operation. After she had come round from the anaesthetic her surgeon talked to her. He was pleased and at the same time surprised. He admitted he had half expected that a hysterectomy would be necessary, as in the majority of such cases, but all that had been required was a 'D and C'.

Valerie had written in her diary after her very first healing, 'an extraordinary unfolding and flowering of spirit. Why?' A possible answer to that question had been emerging since her artistic talent had reawakened in a surprising, new and sometimes very disturbing form.

In the late spring of 1981, soon after a visit to Venice with her husband, she began to do rapid portraits with a sanguine pencil on large drawing pads. But these were not normal portraits. They were not of people she had seen or met. They were 'inspired' in the sense that they just came into her mind and demanded expression. Several of the early ones bore a distinct resemblance to her husband's brother, who had been killed on the Normandy beaches on D Day. One was positively identified as a former patient of Phil's who had died of cancer of the gullet. Valerie had never seen him.

During the next two years she did over 700 such portrait sketches. Her mother took it as perfectly natural that Valerie should be doing psychic art. Her activity was at its most intense during the Falklands campaign. She was in hospital at the time and as her son was out there she felt closely involved. But there was equally urgent activity during the victory parade in the City of London, when one portrait appeared for each of the three services — Army, Navy, Air Force. During the raising of the *Mary Rose* she did many faces which had a sixteenth-century feel. Music has always been a strong stimulus to such drawing. The sketches were done rapidly, sometimes in the dark. They varied in style and had an arresting vividness. Many were repeats, faces which appeared again and again. As time went on she began to write messages on the back of each drawing. Mostly they were in English but sometimes in correct German or Latin, both of which are languages unknown to Valerie.

It is an extraordinary gift which seems to have been activated by healing. The insistence with which her unseen models present themselves for drawing can be a source of stress as well as fulfilment. The whole thing may indicate a form of communication which transcends space and time. But that question still remains unanswered. Why?

PATRICIA BAIN

Disease: Terminal cancer.

'I wish I could go on feeling that for ever.'

Alistair Bain is an administrator at the Tavistock Centre near Swiss Cottage. Social and medical studies are conducted from the Centre. His particular field is groups and the inter-reaction of people on each other. He is in his mid-forties, has a quiet, reflective manner and gives careful consideration before answering questions. He has two children. Lauren his daughter is nine and his son Josh is five.

His wife died in June 1979 when she was thirty-nine years of age. Since her death Alistair has become a student of all things to do with healing and has become especially interested in Buddhism.

His wife Pat first noticed symptoms of cancer in 1977. She underwent an operation in 1978. In 1979 the cancer broke out again. She went into hospital for another operation but was discharged because the illness was terminal. She was taken back to her home to spend the last two weeks of her life there.

A doctor who also worked at the Centre and knew about Phil Edwardes suggested to Alistair that he should try healing. It was not possible to move Pat but fortunately Phil was able to come to North London. He paid his first visit on 25 June.

Pat Bain was fully *compos mentis.* During healing she experienced a tingling sensation in her liver where the cancer was located. A drain attached to her body which had not been functioning before healing now began to work properly. Her pain was relieved, but more important to her was the sense of peace which healing gave her. 'Whatever took place,' Alistair remembers, 'it gave her contentment.'

Phil paid a second visit on 28 June. Pat seemed brighter and more cheerful. She was again fully aware of what was happening and Phil dared to hope that she could be cured. From this healing she derived an even greater sense of happiness and well-being. When it was over she said with deep sincerity, 'I wish I could go on feeling that for ever.'

But the end came two days later. She gave up her spirit on 30 June. As Alistair put it, 'Physically she died.'

JENNY PATTISON

Disease: Diabetes.

'Rather lost and beyond the pale, I was.'

Jenny Pattison lives in Horsham and is married to a chartered accountant who commutes daily to London. She has a daughter of nineteen and a son of sixteen.

At school Jenny did well up till O-level standard but she found A-levels rather beyond her. It was probably because she had no real ambition to go on to university. Her parents were the kind of parents who allowed their children to make up their own minds about their respective careers without pressurizing them. While she was still at school Jenny had begun to think of becoming a nurse. The profession attracted her because it was active both physically and mentally and was 'something I could get my teeth into.'

After the usual interview she became a trainee nurse at St George's Hospital, which was then at Hyde Park Corner. At the end of the three years training she took the usual examinations and qualified as a State Registered Nurse. She had decided by then that she was not really a born nurse. She liked working with the patients but found the procedures difficult to pick up. Almost immediately she married Roger and became involved in running a house and bringing up children.

She had suffered from diabetes since the age of eighteen, but it had been no real trouble until the 1970s when she was in her early thirties. There would be the odd breakdown of her big toes but she got by, often with the help of antibiotics. She went every so often to the doctor to get the antibiotics but on the whole she avoided doctors. In 1975 she had a bad breakdown on her right big toe but she was used to having patches of trouble like that. However, at the end of 1977 she developed a big ulcer under her right foot. It never healed. It would improve for a time and then break down again. By the summer of 1978 she was going every week to her doctor. Finally the little toe of the right foot went gangrenous. She knew she was 'for the chop'.

In September 1978 the surgeon at East Surrey Hospital, Redhill, took off the front half of her right foot in what is known as a mid-tarsal amputation. It healed up pretty well but then the left foot started to give trouble. She developed an abscess inside her ankle which did not manifest itself on the outside. Because of the amputation of her right foot her left foot was taking a lot of strain. She was getting about on crutches, but even so the weight was causing her bones to grate and this led to deterioration. She was 'for the chop again'.

In February 1979 the same surgeon performed a below-knee amputation, that is to say her limb was cut off half-way between the knee and ankle. Of her surgeon she says 'he was super'. The double amputation was not the terrible trauma it might have been. She could still walk with the aid of a stick, thanks to the artificial limb on her left leg. She could drive a car, do all the household work and was not a burden on her family. She was able to plod on. She found that the easiest way to get about the house was on her knees and her family became quite used to seeing her scurrying around in that way.

'Then, blow me! The half foot got an ulcer underneath.'

Under doctor's orders she spent most of the summer of 1979 resting. The foot healed up and was all right until the summer holidays of that year when she had to use it more than usual. Then the foot blew up again. For the first time she felt desperate. She did not want to go to her surgeon because she was afraid of further amputations. Though she had not been bothered by the amputations the fact that her half foot had blown up threw her. It shook her faith in God. Up till then she thought she had done pretty well and that God would give her an approving pat on the back. Instead she was in more trouble. Bewildered and angry she wanted to hit out at God. She swore at him and used all the worst words. She waited defiantly for a thunderbolt to fall. Instead she was led to Phil.

She happened to see an article on Phil Edwardes' healing in the *West Sussex County Times.* Acting swiftly on an impulse she moved to the telephone and found herself dialling his number. Phil listened to what she had to say and replied, 'Can you come tomorrow?'

Next day was a Tuesday. She went alone, not telling anyone, not even her family. She knew nothing about healing but somehow she had faith in him. 'Rather lost and beyond the pale I was.'

Phil's talk meant a lot to her. 'Suddenly it made sense. I saw things in a broader way.' Since that first visit on 2 October 1979 she has been going to him every week with intervals only when she's away on holiday. During this period she has continued to go regularly to her diabetic specialist at Horsham. She has also been in hospital three times. On one occasion one and a half litres of pus was drained out of the leg which had suffered the below-knee amputation.

As far as the ulcer is concerned it still comes and goes but rarely gives serious trouble. However, she is convinced that if she hadn't been going regularly for healing she would be very ill by now, and would most likely have lost the second leg in the same way as the first. Healing to her foot has not been dramatic but is maintaining the *status quo*. The thing that *was* dramatic about the initial healing was the sudden drop in the daily requirement of the insulin dose. When she first went to Phil Edwardes she was taking 28 units of Actrapid and 40 units of Monotard (slow-acting) insulin per day. Gradually the amount of Actrapid which she needed was reduced to 26, 24, 22 and finally down to 8. It now fluctuates between 8 and 20 units according to daily circumstances.

This drop in insulin is a difficult fact to explain away. She feels that most doctors would comment that 'it would have happened anyway' and who can say that they would not be correct? For example her diabetic specialist did not bat an eyelid or appear to think it in any way unusual when she informed him of the change. On the other hand it is significant that the change should have taken place only *after* she had gone for healing. At the time her whole anxiety was centred on the ulcer and the thought that her diabetic condition might be improved never once entered her head. So it was not the result of wishful thinking. Could the pancreas have started to produce a certain amount of its own insulin again having not been able to do so for twenty-one years? It is a question which must remain open but she has come to believe that 'with God all things are possible'.

'What healing has done for me most,' she wrote later, 'has been to open my eyes to a new concept of God, the world and our spiritual life, and to release me from the narrow confines of my erstwhile religious beliefs. I hit out at God in blind frustration and despair, and His response was to lead me to a place where His healing was freely given to body and soul with *no conditions attached.* This then, to me, cannot be the God who, we are taught by the Church, gives us free will with one hand and punishes us with the other if we use the gift wrongly and fail to repent. God's loving answer to my tantrums evoked from me a loving response to Him, and awoke a desire to live in tune with the Creator and his Creation. I feel a wonderful freedom now because I am responding to God of my own *free will* and not because of fear of punishment if I don't or out of a sense of "Christian duty". I firmly believe that healing comes from God. Not everyone, perhaps not me, experiences a miracle cure of the body, but this no longer matters to me, as it is insignificant beside the spiritual release that healing and, not least, contact with Phil has given me.'

★ ★ ★

After reading this book you may wish to enquire personally about healing. If so, please write (enclosing a stamped and addressed envelope) to:

Phil Edwardes
Roundstreet House
Wisborough Green
West Sussex RH14 0AN